THE JOY BEYOND CRAVING

A BUDDHIST PERSPECTIVE ON ADDICTION AND RECOVERY

By Joni Kay Rose, M.Div., CHT

DESERT WORDSMITH PRODUCTIONS

www.desertwordsmith.com
desertwordsmith@yahoo.com

ISBN 0-0729929-0-1

Library of Congress Control Number: 2003091856

Addiction / Buddhism / Meditation / Recovery /
Religion / Self-Help / Title

Rose, Joni Kay
THE JOY BEYOND CRAVING

Acknowledgement: This text was proofread by Judith
Salzman, MCSE, of Digital Mindfulness
www.digitalmindfulness.com

TABLE OF CONTENTS

TABLE OF CONTENTS

INTRODUCTION

"YOU KNOW YOU WANT IT! WHY WAIT? BUY NOW! LOW MONTHLY PAYMENTS ..." Our modern culture daily bombards us with instant-gratification messages. We're continually encouraged to seek out some new form of amusement or find a way to become wealthier. The underlying assumption appears to be, "Get what you can when you can get it, because that's what will make you happy." In effect, material things have become our gods.

Yet are we really happy? We suffer from depression, from insomnia, from mental disorders of various kinds. Above all we suffer from addictions, often becoming addicted to the very things that we do to try to find happiness. We drink, we smoke, we take drugs (legal or illegal), we overeat, we gamble compulsively, we have obsessive-compulsive disorders, we become addicted to sex and romance—or we may even become addicted to religion. And THE MORE WE ENGAGE IN THESE ADDICTIVE BEHAVIOR PATTERNS, THE MORE MISERABLE WE MAKE OURSELVES.

So long as we remain in denial, we may continue to delude ourselves as to the cause of our unhappiness. We may go on believing, as our popular culture teaches us daily, that indulging our little whims will make us feel better. We may pretend, and possibly even try to convince ourselves, that we're living successful and fulfilling lives, when deep down we feel empty and miserable.

Eventually, though, we have to come to terms with our reality. Usually this happens as a result of a crisis we encounter, like losing a job or failing in business as a result of our dysfunctional behavior patterns.

In my own experience, I've spent decades trying to find peace and happiness by attempting to fulfill my desires through various physical and metaphysical means. Invariably I found only frustration in the end. I seldom got what I truly wanted; and even when I did it simply led to more craving and dissatisfaction. Only when I examined and dealt with the very process of craving itself did I begin to find peace of mind. This I have done mainly through my study of Buddhism, which plays a major role in this book.

While Buddhism is in certain respects unique among the world's religions—in the teaching of the nonexistence of the soul, for instance—the basic Buddhist teachings are otherwise generally compatible with other great religious teachings. The causal connection between desire and suffering, for instance, is found in some Hindu texts, and no doubt has a common origin in Indian teachings that predated the Buddha. We can also find echoes of these teachings in the sayings of Jesus, especially regarding the emphasis on living an upright and unselfish life. It would be difficult to find anything in Jesus' own teachings that contradicts these principles in any significant way.

INTRODUCTION

Though many of the Buddha's teachings have parallels in other religions, the systematic way in which he taught the causal relationship between craving and suffering is a little less open to confusion. Judaism, Christianity, and Islam place more emphasis on history—certain things are asserted to have happened in the past and affect the present; and certain things are expected to happen in the future. While some people may find these prophecies comforting, in this context they can be distracting from our focus on how addiction arises and how it is to be overcome.

These religions also are more likely to encourage the notion of separation of "believers" from "nonbelievers." Although this may not have been the original intent of this dichotomy, it can be misused to foster self-righteousness or moral superiority. We want to begin by focusing on the issue of how addictive desire arises, what it does to all of us, and how to overcome it. That is precisely the issue that the Buddha dealt with in his Four Noble Truths, which we'll look at in Part 1.

This isn't an attempt to convert everyone to Buddhism. Such proselytizing isn't encouraged in most forms of Buddhism anyway. Rather than urging people to give up their previous religions and become Buddhists, I'd like to help them see the Buddha's teachings as universal principles that are compatible with the teachings of all true religions.

Another important component of my own life has been my experience as an addict in recovery. I've been active in recovery meetings for nearly as long as I've been seriously studying

Buddhism. The Twelve-Step model used in these meetings centers around turning one's life over to a Higher Power, that is to say, God. This might seem at variance with Buddhism, which is often thought to encourage personal effort and self-sufficiency. Yet in fact the two are not far apart at all, as we'll see.

The real contrast lies between the popular culture of our times, be it of the materialistic or "metaphysical" bent, and truth that has stood the test of time for more than two millennia. The Buddhist teachings and the Twelve-Step process both help us understand that it is the very process of craving that we most need to overcome. We'll take a look at each of these in turn.

PART 1: THE FOUR NOBLE TRUTHS

If we were to sum up the prevailing message of our culture, the result might look something like this:

1. It is normal to be happy and experience pleasure. Everyone has a right to a happy and pleasure-filled life.
2. The way to happiness lies in fulfilling your desires.
3. If you are unhappy the cause must lie in blocks, whether internal or external, to your getting what you want.
4. Therefore the key to happiness lies in overcoming the obstacles that prevent you from experiencing pleasure and getting what you want.

There are many variations to these premises; but ordinarily the key assumptions are that happiness is normal and that we can attain it by getting what we want. The goal could be anything from wealth and power to eternal life; but it's seen as a goal that is or should be available to all. Happiness and pleasure are rarely distinguished from each other.

A little over 2500 years ago there lived in India a famous sage who taught essentially the opposite of this. Though the words attributed to Siddhartha Gautama, known to history as the Enlightened One or the Buddha, have filled many books, four of his teachings are so important they are called the Four Noble Truths:

1. Life by its very nature is unsatisfactory, and suffering is found everywhere. All of us experience pain and sorrow in our lives, and in time we will all grow old, become infirm, and die.
2. The reason all of us suffer is that we're full of all kinds of self-centered cravings, to which we are bound by attachment (in other words, they're addictions), so that we're never satisfied. In the end our very efforts to seek more and more satisfaction for ourselves are certain to create more suffering.
3. If we want to find liberation from our suffering we must first learn to let go of these addictive cravings which are the cause of our suffering in the first place.
4. There is a path that offers a way out of our addictive craving and hence leads to liberation from suffering. Based on correct understanding and motivation, rigorous ethical self-discipline, and effortful and mindful contemplation, the way out of suffering is called the Eightfold Path. The eight aspects of this Path are Right Understanding, Right Aspiration, Right Speech, Right Action, Right Livelihood, Right Effort, Right Mindfulness, and Right Concentration.

The word "Noble" is a free translation of the Sanskrit word "Arya." While in some forms of Hinduism the concept of "Arya" has taken on a caste-related interpretation, the Buddha repeatedly insisted it really has nothing to do with ancestry, but is based on one's dedication to practicing the Dharma, the way of awareness. We could just as well call them the Four Holy Truths, unless the word Holy might cause some people to see them as commandments. We might even call them the Four Basic Truths, since understanding them thoroughly is essential to true spiritual progress in Buddhism. The Buddha intended the Four Noble Truths as guideposts to his followers in their lives, in order to help people overcome addictive craving that leads to suffering. But nowadays not all Buddhists take them seriously as a guide to daily living. All over the world people bow before statues of the Buddha, read flowery passages attributed to him, and even cast spells in his name. Yet only a minority of Buddhists, whether "Eastern" or "Western," actually study, live, and practice the Four Noble Truths that were the original cornerstone of his teaching.

Rarely is attention paid to the process of addiction and recovery in most modern Buddhist denominations. A few even encourage devotees to pray for material as well as spiritual benefits for themselves and their families. Though Buddhism was designed to help people learn to overcome addictive desire, it has so far not adapted well to the needs of people living in a complex society ruled by craving.

While there are some rigorous texts available on the Four Noble Truths and the Eightfold Path, after numerous translations many of them are dull, technical, and hard to follow. Understanding them can be a challenge; and trying to relate them to everyday life in the twenty-first century is beyond many of us. Hence despite years of Buddhist practice, students and sometimes even teachers of Buddhism often have to turn to Twelve-Step meetings or other outside assistance in order to avoid destroying ourselves with our addictions of various kinds. Yet the Four Noble Truths were originally intended to help people overcome the addictive cravings that create unhappiness in our lives. If we systematically live these Truths, we learn there is a way out of our suffering. These teachings can thus be of immense benefit to people of all faiths, including many Buddhists who have never really studied them systematically.

Since the Four Noble Truths are, like the Twelve Steps, sequential, it's best to examine them in order, one at a time, making sure we fully understand each one before we move on to the next. Let's do that now.

THE FIRST NOBLE TRUTH: LIFE IS A BITCH, AND THEN YOU DIE!

Life is a bowl of cherries, a beach, a blast, an endless party! So teaches our popular culture. Those people who are suffering, who are in pain, who are poor, who are depressed, or who are disabled—they just need to get with the program. Come on everyone; let's lighten up and have fun!

But there's another side to this, also found in our popular culture, and it harmonizes perfectly with the Buddha's First Noble Truth: "Life is a bitch, and then you die!" Of course those aren't the Buddha's own words—he didn't even speak English; yet it amounts to about the same thing. The Universe is impossibly screwed up, and whatever can go wrong most likely will, and probably at the worst possible moment. This is Murphy's Law; for Murphy, consciously or otherwise, must have known the First Noble Truth.

Whereas some other religions and philosophies teach that the universe is perfect and suffering is either unnecessary or illusory, the Buddha began by saying that suffering happens to all of us. The Pali word attributed to him in the sutras is DUKKHA, which means not only suffering, but also disjointedness, pain, unpleasantness, or lack of satisfaction. Pali is the ancient Indian language in which the earliest Buddhist sutras were written down.

While this teaching may seem pessimistic, it's designed to confront the true nature of our existence. Buddhism is a religion that begins by looking at reality as it is, rather than how we think it ought to be. WHETHER WE LIKE IT OR NOT, SUFFERING IS OMNIPRESENT. We are born in pain. Many of the world's people don't get enough to eat. Even in these supposedly prosperous United States of America there are millions with no place to live, unable to meet the necessities of life.

Even among the minority of people who are truly wealthy, there's no guarantee of happiness that comes with the Ferrari and the swimming pool. We can struggle all our lives and finally make it into the jet set, only to find it an empty triumph. All our lives, no matter how wealthy and powerful some of us may become, there will always be something we want but can't have no matter how hard we try to get it. In any case, money can't buy peace of mind, as studies have shown.

Many of us also suffer from physical or mental disorders, or both. Some people suffer from the long-term effects of a head or spinal injury that may have occurred decades ago. Or we may have fibromyalgia, or serious allergies, or cancer, or AIDS, or sensitivity to the chemicals that abound in our world.

Whether we are rich or poor, whether we are young or old, whether we are able-bodied or paralyzed, eventually all of us must learn that life really hurts. At some point all of us will, as the Buddha said, be separated from what we love and forced to live with what we detest. And in the end, unless like James Dean we die young and make a beautiful corpse, all of us will grow old, become infirm, and die. Like it or not, that's what life is like. Deep in our hearts, all of us can hear the cosmic scream.

Like many people I have suffered with chronic depression much of my life. If someone tells me there's no need to be depressed because the universe is just perfect as it is and it's all God's Plan unfolding, I'm afraid such talk won't help me feel less depressed. It could even make me feel worse.

If on the other hand someone reminds me that my depression shows my awareness of the Noble Truth of suffering and is quite normal, I may begin to feel a little bit better. In fact, when I feel depressed I usually tell myself something of the sort, and it does seem to help.

Actually depression can be a good opportunity to study the First Noble Truth. In a way depression is a kind of heightened awareness of the omnipresence of suffering. If we can avoid trying to escape into illusion or fantasy, it can be a great teacher.

The problem with depression isn't necessarily that we exaggerate the suffering. Rather there may be a tendency to identify with it, to pretend that nothing in the universe suffers as you do. If you open your eyes and see, you will realize that it's not just you who am suffering; for the whole universe suffers with you.

Yet what do most of us actually do when we come face to face with suffering? We medicate ourselves, don't we? We reach for our drug of choice, be it liquor, tobacco, marijuana, cocaine, heroin, tranquilizers, Prozac, food, sex, gambling, television, or even rambling conversation. We DO something to take our minds off the pain.

Perhaps this is understandable. We don't want to experience our suffering, so we take or do something to distract ourselves from it. Unfortunately whatever relief we get in this way is only temporary at best; and most of the "drugs" we use will create more problems for us later, thus worsening our suffering in the long run.

What usually happens is that we find we need more and more of our chosen substance or pastime to relieve the suffering, until it just doesn't work anymore. Now we need it just to stay alive, or at least we feel we do. Thus the addictive cycle deepens our suffering.

The First Noble Truth suggests that instead of medicating ourselves to keep from feeling the suffering, we might go ahead and live with it a while, maybe even embrace it, and try to see what it's all about. Thich Nhat Hanh, a well-known Vietnamese Zen author and teacher, might say we can say hello to our suffering, and maybe nurture it as though it were a crying baby. At least then we won't be running from it anymore. And then it may be possible to understand what causes suffering.

In doing this practice the idea is not to concentrate only on your own suffering, but to look around you and see how omnipresent it is. Thus from the very start you can begin to get beyond your insular self-concept to see that it's not my suffering or your suffering or someone else's suffering; it's just suffering, and it's everywhere.

Should you try to delude yourself into thinking no one suffers the way you do, the universe will show you there are others far worse off. If you complain that you can't afford a decent pair of shoes, you will soon meet someone with no feet—even if it's a snake. We need to stop identifying personally with suffering and realize it's something we all experience.

This exemplifies the challenge that we all face, as the Buddha explained it. You have created the delusion that you are a separate being, with your own private issues. That delusion inevitably leads to suffering. When you realize that in truth there is no "you" to be stuck in your suffering, deliverance in near at hand. The best way to do this is to become aware of all the suffering around you.

For those of us who are addicts—and nearly everybody is addicted to something—this is an especially valuable practice. For it's our unwillingness to confront suffering that has caused us to seek solace in our addictive habits, whatever they are. Usually this results in yet more suffering, so that the cycle deepens. Some people have even contracted incurable diseases like AIDS as a result of their addictive behavior patterns.

"We admitted we were powerless over our addiction, that our lives had become unmanageable." It is this unmanageability that points to the Noble Truth of suffering. It's the first step in our ongoing journey toward enlightenment.

When we look around us it may seem that the universe is unfair. Innocent people keep suffering, while selfish people profit from the exploitation of others. The First Noble Truth reminds us that everyone suffers—the rich as well as the poor, and the seemingly innocent as well as the guilty. The question is, why is there all this suffering in the world?

THE SECOND NOBLE TRUTH: IF YOU THINK YOU HAVE TO HAVE IT, THEN IT REALLY HAS YOU!

Buddha's Second Noble Truth is a little harder for Americans, maybe people in general, to understand. Most of us can see that suffering is all-pervasive; but looking into its causes is a little beyond most of us. We may be tempted to believe we suffer due to not getting what we want. Few of us seem to have the insight to see that IT IS THE VERY EXPERIENCE OF WANTING THAT LIES AT THE ROOT OF SUFFERING.

If we look closely, we can see this is true on both an individual and a societal level. We each bring suffering on ourselves by our incessant desires, to which we readily become attached. Indeed, our very efforts to achieve happiness by satisfying our desires most often lead to yet more suffering.

Likewise we bring suffering on others by our lack of compassion and understanding: by oppressing others, putting them down, pushing them out of our way, and generally mistreating them. And the consequences of these karmic actions come back to us when others treat us the same way.

To make matters worse, we live in a society that encourages us to be acquisitive, competitive, and oftentimes at odds with our fellow human beings. Constantly we're bombarded with messages to fulfill our cravings, get ahead of others, and be at the top of the pecking order. Thus collectively through our efforts to satisfy our desires at all costs, even to the detriment of other people, we bring suffering on all people.

When people talk about addiction, they often think it's synonymous with substance abuse: addiction to alcohol, tobacco, marijuana, amphetamines, narcotics, painkillers, prescription drugs, or food. Yet actually substance abuse is only one form of addiction. We can just as well be addicted to sex, to violence, to gambling, to watching television, to owning fancy cars, to having lots of money, or even to certain forms of religion. All these involve obsessive-compulsive behavior patterns that are just as difficult to overcome as drinking, if not more so.

Sometimes these "process" addictions are regarded as "psychological" rather than "chemical" addictions. Yet there's a psychological aspect to alcoholism as well as a chemical component. And some process addictions such as sexual obsession or compulsive gambling involve the creation of chemicals within the body as part of the "high" that's created while engaged in the addictive activity. We thus become chemically as well as psychologically addicted to the hormones that the body itself manufactures.

The Pali word for desire used in the Buddhist sutras is TANHA, which literally means "thirst". That ought to have significance to alcoholics. While TANHA is sometimes translated as "desire," it's a special kind of desire. TANHA refers to the grasping, self-centered wanting that comes with attachment to the object of desire. One English equivalent we could use is craving. Other words might be clinging, attachment, obsession, compulsion, or addiction.

As the Buddha taught, ignorance lies at the root of the problem. No doubt all of us truly want to be happy. Yet through our ignorance the very efforts we make to satisfy our desire for happiness are based on craving, and thus instead result in more suffering for ourselves and others. Then, as all addicts know from our experience, we try yet harder to satisfy our desires, until the effort becomes compulsive; and we continue in this cycle long after we might otherwise have been able to see that we're sinking deeper and deeper into addiction and suffering.

In Buddhist teachings, the suffering that results from TANHA manifests itself even beyond physical death, so that our greed in this life can cause suffering in a future life. Indeed the very process of rebirth is said to be driven by the results of the karmic choices made in one's previous life. Based on ignorance, we make unwise choices that result in our minds and bodies, and hence our feelings, creating the experience of craving. Craving in turn results in clinging, so that our entire existence becomes permeated with this grasping nature. This in turn causes us to be reborn into yet more suffering, old age, and death.

This causal relationship among the twelve links in the chain of suffering is described in the Buddhist principle of Dependent Origination. Some of the teachings seem dry and technical, and of course it's more difficult to perceive the predicted effect on future lives. This is especially true when the discussion delves into possible rebirth in heavens, hells, or the realm of the hungry ghosts. Yet if we look carefully we can see the result of our actions and feelings within our present life-span, without even worrying about possible future lives.

Buddhist sutras mention three kinds of TANHA. First is the desire for sensual pleasures like food, sex, or excitement. Then there is ambition, the desire to become something, to achieve greatness or to be a leader. Finally there is aversion, the desire to get rid of what we don't like, such as anger, jealousy, or even our ego.

The first of these three forms of craving is the most obvious. Most of us are undoubtedly obsessed with sensual desire; our culture teaches us to cater to it. We eat and drink, not to fulfill our body's nutritional needs, but to satisfy our cravings. We seek sensation, excitement, and of course, sexual pleasure.

How very few of us have learned to distinguish between momentary sensual pleasures and true spiritual joy or bliss! Addicts often blame ourselves for our poor impulse control, but actually most everyone in our society has this problem in some form or another. We're all obsessed with satisfying our every little whim.

The second form of craving, which we might call ambition, is a little subtler. After all, what can be wrong with wanting to achieve, to be a success, to get ahead, maybe even to be enlightened? Clearly nothing, just as there is nothing wrong with hunger and thirst. Yet when this becomes an all-consuming obsession with achieving our goals, however lofty, then it too will lead to more suffering.

As for spiritual attainment, if you want to be enlightened so you can impress others and become a renowned teacher, then this also is a form of ambition that will lead only to more suffering. Buddha's cousin Devadatta had this problem, and it destroyed him. There have been many others since then; and the temptation is there for all of us, however well-meaning. In recovery programs, similarly, we're warned to sponsor other addicts because it helps us in our own recovery, not to pretend we know the answers and can show them "The Way."

Aversion, the third form of craving, is perhaps yet subtler. We may genuinely want to get rid of certain unpleasant aspects of our lives; but if we're attached to this desire it too can be a form of TANHA. We want to overcome our negative traits, perhaps even get rid of our ego. Why do we want to do this? So we will achieve more and feel superior to others, or why? Unless we're truly humble in our aspiration, we had best be wary. The Buddha taught his followers to let go of craving, not to try to vanquish it like an enemy to be triumphed over.

Likewise in our recovery programs we're cautioned not to expect to suddenly get rid of our addictions; rather we need to patiently learn to turn aside from them. We've wanted to sober up for so long, but somehow we can't seem to make it stick until we do our step-work. That's why it often doesn't work to try to "white-knuckle" ourselves away from our addictions: because our very motivation is based on aversion, another form of TANHA.

Buddhism is sometimes stereotyped as an other-worldly "Eastern" religion that teaches we must give up all desire. We've already seen that Buddhism in fact offers practical solutions to the dilemmas of everyday life. The Buddha advocated the "Middle Way" between self-indulgence and extreme asceticism, both of which he himself had previously experienced and then rejected. In this instance, Buddhism doesn't teach that we must overcome all desire; rather it suggests that we look carefully at our desires to see what they're like.

There's another word for desire in Pali. That word is SANKAPPA, which is variously translated as aspiration, intention, conviction, determination, or even thought. SANKAPPA might be considered positive desire: a heartfelt wish to serve all beings in the most effective way possible. All Buddhists are encouraged to practice SANKAPPA, as it's the second component of the Eightfold Path.

When we say, "May all beings be happy," or "May I be enlightened for the sake of all beings," we're practicing SANKAPPA. Even if you pray for your own enlightenment, it's out of a wish to serve others unselfishly. SANKAPPA is free from attachment. When you pray for the happiness of all beings, you hopefully won't get upset when you look around and see there's still much misery in the world. That just offers you more of a challenge to face in your life's work.

TANHA, by contrast, is selfish, grasping, addictive craving. Even if a desire starts out as a preference, if it's selfish in nature eventually it's likely to create an attachment, and you may get frustrated if you can't satisfy it. Thus by its very nature craving creates suffering, both for oneself and for others. This distinction, between our petty self-centered desires, or TANHA, and our heart's desire to serve others, or SANKAPPA, is essential to understanding the Second Noble Truth.

Unfortunately when most of us look honestly at the bulk of our desires, we can usually see that they're cravings, not aspirations. Much of the time we're selfish or at least self-centered in our motivation, in the sense that on some level we want to advance ourselves above other people or prove our superiority over them. To make matters worse, when we don't get our way, which is more often than not the case, we become upset or frustrated.

In understanding ourselves it's essential that we look closely at our desires, to winnow out the true aspirations we feel in our spirit from the immense mass of self-centered craving that afflicts us moment by moment. Which of our desires are unselfish, caring, compassionate, and free from attachment? Only those are aspirations to be cultivated; the rest are but cravings to be set aside.

The distinction between craving and aspiration is especially important to recovering addicts. In Twelve-Step terms it might be seen as the difference between addiction and willingness. If we understand this distinction we can see that it's not just a question of what we're addicted to; it's the difference between addictive craving and selfless aspiration.

If we addictively crave anything, even going to heaven or becoming enlightened, it's going to cause suffering. If we instead turn to our true aspirations, with the aid of our Higher Consciousness we can overcome our addictive cravings.

Sometimes people lament that despite our so-called prosperity so many Americans suffer from depression, or at least confusion. Yet if we observe that the primary motivation for most people in our society is greed, it becomes understandable that many Americans are unhappy.

In any case, there are millions of Americans, not to mention people in most other countries, who still live in want. The enormous disparity of wealth in this and other countries is itself a result of selfish greed, and continues to create more suffering for all. If we all truly cared for each other and ourselves, we would share our resources and all would prosper without accumulating more than we need.

These Buddhist teachings are in direct contradiction to the prevailing myths of our culture. On a daily basis we're all conditioned to fulfill our desires, however petty. You feel like having some chocolate ice cream? Go ahead and indulge! We're so accustomed to fulfilling our little cravings that we can't see the destructive pattern we're getting caught in.

Not only do we desire more and more goods and services, but all these things make our lives increasingly complicated, thus adding to our stress. Computers, watches, and cars may be faster and more sophisticated in what they can do for us. But then we find we need special training to operate these gadgets properly. And the pace of our lives keeps increasing as we expect ourselves to accomplish more and more in less and less time.

The Internet, for instance, is a convenient tool for millions of people. Yet many people have become addicted to it to the extent they spend hours in front of the computer, missing sleep and work and destroying family relationships. People enter chat rooms only to get flamed by others who verbally abuse them. Having an E-mail address leaves one vulnerable to receiving vast quantities of unwanted spam. Worst of all, hate groups use the Internet to propagate their cruel falsehoods.

With all our technological advances, many people are just as self-centered, compulsive, unethical, and hateful as ever; and most will continue to be that way so long as they know only how to satisfy their own desires without regard for others. The issue is not between Buddhism versus Christianity, or even between "Eastern" versus "Western" philosophies—as if there were a dividing line between "The East" and "The West" that could be found somewhere on a map of Asia! The real contrast lies between our popular consumer-oriented culture and timeless spiritual truth that has been handed down over the centuries.

The causal link between craving and suffering is one of the most valuable teachings of the Buddha. Once we appreciate this knowledge we can feel gratitude, rather than frustration, when we don't get what we want or we get what we don't want.

So long as the universe keeps giving you what you want, you can maintain the illusion that you're in charge of your life, maybe even that you can control the universe. When you can't get what you want no matter how hard you try, this is the opportunity to look at your motivations to see how craving creates suffering in you and others. Thus you may see your entire experience, including disappointment, as an opportunity to learn the true nature of desire.

THE THIRD NOBLE TRUTH: NIRVANA IS THE JOY OF BEING WHERE YOU ARE AND LOVING WHAT IS HERE AND NOW!

We've seen that suffering is all-pervasive, and that we cause it, individually and collectively, by craving what we don't have and clinging to what we do have. It follows logically from this that to find true happiness we need to let go of our attachments, to get beyond our craving and clinging nature. Such a simple argument this is! Yet it's so difficult to put into practice when our addictive nature, encouraged by the popular media, keeps fooling us into thinking we can find happiness in striving to fulfill our cravings.

Still, if we contemplate the situation carefully we can see the truth: WE CAN NEVER BE 100% HAPPY BY TRYING TO GET WHATEVER WE WANT. ONLY BY BEING CONTENT WITH WHAT WE HAVE WILL WE FIND TRUE JOY AND BLISS.

Some people will try to tell you that you can have anything you want if you truly believe you can have it. Do you want eternal life in heaven? Maybe you can have that; maybe you can't. No one truly knows for sure, so we'd better not count on it. Do you want to grow old, become infirm, and die? Unless you die young, that's exactly what will happen to you, regardless of what affirmations you may make.

So long as you keep trying to get your way, even if you use "metaphysical" techniques to try to impose your will on the universe, you will simply reinforce your self-concept of an ego. Thus you'll remain stuck in your suffering, whether or not you appear to succeed in getting what you want.

ONLY BY LETTING GO OF YOUR ADDICTIVE DESIRES CAN YOU FIND EVER-LASTING PEACE AND JOY. You and I have spent enough time and energy trying to impose our egotistical little wills on the Universe. Bliss is found not in plotting future "prosperity," but in living in the moment all the time.

Of course we may still have goals in life; but the idea is not to be attached to them, since things rarely turn out the way we want in any case. This again is to cultivate aspiration rather than craving in ourselves. With no attachment to the results of our actions we can enjoy the results if we succeed, but if we fail we can merely shrug it off and move on. Thus we can find serenity no matter what the outcome of our efforts.

Note that we're not trying to get rid of our ego-based desires by stamping them out, pushing them away, repressing them, or even suppressing them. That would be aversion, which as we've seen is itself another form of craving. We acknowledge that we feel what we feel, and then we let go of those feelings so we won't continue to bring suffering upon ourselves. This is a gentle, relaxed process that we need to practice at all times, as desires come upon us continually and need to be let go of all the time.

In a way the all-pervasive nature of suffering is an excellent teacher, as it constantly reminds us that we have to let go of our attachments if we want to be happy. If we focus on what is happening right now and what we need to do right now, there's no room for worry or fear or even doubt. Then there truly is bliss. This is what the Third Noble Truth has to teach us.

Ken Keyes, the author of the HANDBOOK TO HIGHER CONSCIOUSNESS, was a quadriplegic. Yet he was one of the happiest people I've ever met, always smiling, never complaining about the fact that he couldn't even maneuver his own wheelchair. Life, as Ken described it, is a cornucopia if you simply enjoy what you have and don't bemoan what you can't have. You can do that by overcoming all your addictions, even your addiction to something as mundane as wanting people to treat you courteously. With no attachments to things being a certain way, you can be completely happy all the time.

Though traditional schools of Buddhism sometimes seem to imply that NIRVANA is an all-or-nothing event, nowadays many Buddhists see enlightenment as a process. Thus we are forever learning how to overcome our addictive traps and free ourselves from the bondage of the self we've concocted. It's a lifelong journey.

Still, NIRVANA isn't merely the overcoming of the various self-centered cravings you experience. It's letting go of your whole concept of your "self," your attachment to being who you think you are. It's getting beyond this character you've concocted in your imagination and then identified with, and just seeing what is, without the illusion of an unchanging individual "self." If you've created an image of yourself as a saintly, enlightened being, even that has to go. IT IS ONLY IN LETTING GO OF ALL YOUR SELF-CONCEPTS THAT YOU CAN FIND TRUE FREEDOM.

NIRVANA is a Sanskrit word; the Pali equivalent is NIBBANA. NIBBANA is also called NIRODHA, the cessation of suffering. Sometimes NIRODHA is misinterpreted to mean the annihilation of self. What it really means is the letting go of the illusion that you have an individual "self" in the first place. Thus you realize that you are pure Beingness. In Twelve Step terms, you stop defying your Higher Power, or trying to bargain with your Higher Power to get "your" way, and realize that your Higher Power is your only true Self.

Isn't it ironic than to find true bliss and peace of mind, what you really need to give up is your "self"! Instead of trying to find happiness by accumulating more possessions, degrees, titles, or relationships, what you really need to do is give up this identity you've worked so hard to construct. What could be more blissful than to realize at last that there is really no "me" that needs to be defended from attack, no "me" that has to be maintained in the presence of others? That is indeed to experience Oneness with the universe.

THE THIRD NOBLE TRUTH

When Buddhists speak of NIRVANA as emptiness, they're not talking about nothingness or non-being. They're referring instead to the universe as it really is, apart from all the identities, labels and categories we all keep putting on it. Among those identities are you and I as we each have imagined ourselves to be. Emptiness is the pure Beingness that we experience after we drop all our games. In a way Emptiness is another word for God, the Ground of Being.

The Buddha himself gave up his kingdom, his family, his marriage, and all his wealth. In part this may have been because he felt he needed to experience suffering personally. But also he realized he needed to get away from worldly distractions that might have brought him back into the cycle of craving and suffering.

In any case, although the Third Noble Truth states that by overcoming craving we can get beyond suffering and experience NIRVANA, the Buddha chose not to stop here. He wanted a systematic method by which people can do that. This is where the Fourth Noble Truth comes in, the Eightfold Path. We'll look at this next.

THE FOURTH NOBLE TRUTH: THERE IS A WAY!

While Buddhist philosophy can seem enormously complicated, the Buddha wanted to present a few simple principles and techniques that anyone could understand. Thus the Fourth Noble Truth is the same as the Eightfold Path: Right Understanding, Right Intention, Right Speech, Right Action, Right Livelihood, Right Effort, Right Mindfulness, and Right Concentration. Unlike the Four Noble Truths, these eight factors aren't necessarily sequential; they're guidelines to follow simultaneously in our lives. Still, it's easiest to look at them in the order Buddha presented them.

The factors are grouped into three categories. Right Understanding and Right Intention make up the WISDOM portion of the Path. Right Speech, Right Action, and Right Livelihood constitute the ETHICAL portion of the Path. And Right Effort, Right Mindfulness, and Right Concentration form the CONTEMPLATIVE aspect of the Path. Each one supports the others.

The First component of the Eightfold Path is RIGHT UNDERSTANDING. This implies correct understanding of the Four Noble Truths. Buddha liked to cross-reference his teachings like this, to help us comprehend them. So part of our journey on the Eightfold Path is to make sure we understand the Noble Truth of the universality of suffering, the Noble Truth that suffering is caused by attachment to craving, and the Noble Truth that to achieve freedom from suffering we need to let go of craving. By following this understanding we replace delusion with wisdom. Thus we'll want to seek out a means by which we can learn to overcome suffering by letting go of craving; and we'll be attracted to the Eightfold Path, the way out of suffering.

The second component of the Eightfold Path is RIGHT INTENTION or RIGHT ASPIRATION. Having an accurate understanding of how the universe operates, we need to have a proper motivation for our spiritual journey. As we've already noted, this form of aspiration—SANKAPPA in Pali—is based on a heartfelt wish for the happiness of all beings. It must be clearly distinguished from TANHA: craving, ambition, aversion and other forms of desire that are self-centered, emotion-based, and addictive.

Together, Right Understanding and Right Aspiration make up the WISDOM portion of the Eightfold Path. They guide us in understanding correctly how the universe works and how to set our goals accordingly. They also help us overcome delusion, greed, and aversion, which are known as the Three Defilements.

The next three components of the Eightfold Path, Right Speech, Right Action, and Right Livelihood, are the ETHICAL aspect of the Path. They help us lead our lives so as to not create more suffering for ourselves and others. RIGHT SPEECH in Buddhist morality implies abstaining from harmful speech. There are said to be four kinds of harmful speech: lying or false speech, slanderous speech, unnecessarily harsh speech, and idle chatter.

LYING, the first of these, is the most serious. We're asked to avoid making statements that we know to be untrue, since such speech is always destructive. This gets a little trickier as our awareness increases and we begin to see how much of our world is built on falsehood. We're constantly barraged with manipulative advertising and propaganda.

On a personal level, many of us habitually say whatever is expedient at the moment, regardless of whether or not it is true. This is because we've been conditioned to believe we're individual beings with separate self-existences, which is a mistaken belief that Buddhism helps us overcome. There really are no white lies. The only purpose in giving false information is to deceive another person for one's own perceived short-term gain or convenience.

In a world based on lies, the most revolutionary act any of us can take is to tell the truth at all times. In the short run, you may pay a price. You may not be able to get such a high-paying job, and you may lose friends and loved ones. But in the long run you'll see that relationships based on falsehood can't last; and if you lie to get a job you almost certainly won't do well or be happy with it. Truth has its price, but it's worth it in the end, because it breaks down the false barrier of selfhood.

SLANDEROUS SPEECH is a little trickier, as we may truly believe what we say; yet our underlying purpose in saying it can be malicious, and our words may distort the truth to suit our self-centered purposes. Much of the propaganda we encounter daily, particularly in the political realm or in some forms of advertising, involves people trying to prove themselves or their product "right" or superior to others, while putting others down. So we must be careful in examining our true motives before we speak, to be sure that we have no wish to harm others, put people down, distort reality, manipulate others, prove our superiority, or create enmity among people.

HARSH SPEECH is still subtler, as there may be times when we need to speak unpleasant truths in order to be honest. Yet here again we must be sure we're not speaking out of anger. There's already more than enough antagonism in our world; we don't want to add to it.

In many cases our unwise words may come out on the spur of the moment. Hence we always need to think, and if necessary calm down, before we speak. Three examples of harsh speech we might want to avoid are abusive speech, insult, and sarcasm.

While seemingly relatively harmless, IDLE CHATTER OR GOSSIP is the most difficult kind of wrong speech to avoid. If we examine what many of us say in any given day we may see that most of it is unnecessary. We often speak just to hear our own voices.

If we can teach ourselves to be still and listen, we will open ourselves up to other people's perspectives. If the people we're listening to are sensitive, they'll respect us for our silence.

Twelve Step Meetings and similar support groups are wonderful opportunities to practice Right Speech. The rule against crosstalk keeps each member from attacking other members of the group. But you can still get away with saying negative things about people who aren't present, or just talking idly about various experiences unrelated to your addiction.

Yet if you keep your sharing focused on how you feel, and avoid manipulative, slanderous, or abusive speech, as well as unnecessary rambling into irrelevant topics, your share will be of maximum benefit to you as well as to others. And when others share, you can support them by staying silent and listening attentively.

RIGHT ACTION means trying to act so as to avoid causing harm to other beings. Three kinds of actions are specifically to be avoided: intentionally taking the life of a human or animal, taking what is not given, and sexual misconduct.

Killing a human or animal intentionally is perhaps the most serious transgression, to be avoided at all costs. Accidental killing is less serious. Each of us will probably accidentally step on at least one insect each day; such things can't be helped. Yet if we have the true intention of harmlessness, and we try to save the lives of all living things as best we possibly can, there is no serious karmic fault in this.

Next is stealing, or otherwise taking what is not given. We are never to take anything that doesn't belong to us or isn't offered to us. Such behavior only adds to our delusion of being a separate "self" who can profit at the expense of others. Crime really doesn't pay in the long run.

Sexual misconduct implies entering into a sexual liaison in which someone may be hurt. Rape, adultery, and incest are some common examples of sexual behavior to be carefully avoided. Married people are asked to be faithful to their spouses. And except in some forms of Japanese Zen, monks and nuns are required to be completely sexually abstinent.

A few Buddhist teachers may have also condemned homosexuality, and possibly even premarital sex. Yet in general Buddhism makes no judgment about such behavior, which many Buddhists regard as harmless and normal. Nothing can be considered immoral in Buddhism unless it harms someone.

The dilemma with Right Action is that some of us are addicted to the very behaviors we're advised to avoid. In my experience, though, if we follow Right Action as best we can, at least in the areas of our lives where we're able to exert some self-control, it will increase our ability to manage our addictive behavior patterns. Meanwhile attending recovery meetings helps us get beyond our addiction, so that over time we can be restored to sobriety.

RIGHT LIVELIHOOD extends Right Action into the realm of vocation. Here again monks and nuns are more restricted as to the work they may do. For laypeople the ideal is to choose an occupation that doesn't involve killing, dishonesty, or sexual misconduct.

Some traditional examples of occupations to be avoided include butchery, prostitution, using or selling weapons, selling liquor or intoxicants of any kind, making or selling poisons, and practicing usury. The Buddha required military followers to leave their ranks and find another occupation. Though today there are undoubtedly Buddhists in the armed and police forces, such occupations are marginal at best to maintaining Right Livelihood. In fact any occupation involving work that contradicts our deepest moral values is one we might consider changing.

Many of us face a challenge in our occupational choices. If you're a lawyer, you may choose to get rich by working for the wealthy and powerful; or you can choose to live a modest lifestyle offering your knowledge to poor people who most need your help. The decisions we make show where our real values lie.

The final three components of the Eightfold Path, Right Effort, Right Mindfulness, and Right Concentration are grouped together as the SAMADHI or CONTEMPLATIVE components. The first of these, RIGHT EFFORT, is more or less self-explanatory. The idea is to try to prevent or overcome self-centered states of mind, and instead to encourage and nurture unselfishness and compassion in ourselves. Meditation is of great help here, and we need to practice the equanimity we learn during meditation throughout our everyday lives.

In the Twelve-Step Recovery process, even though we've turned our lives and our will over to the care of our Higher Consciousness, we still need to make the effort toward our recovery, in partnership with our Higher Consciousness. And in Step Twelve we learn to reach out to others and share our recovery with them.

RIGHT MINDFULNESS is an especially important component of the Eightfold Path. Mindfulness is to be practiced on a moment-to-moment basis at all times, so as to keep us centered in the here and now. This is one of the reasons we practice sitting and walking meditation, to learn to be present in the moment. Once we become in the habit of being mindful, it can be carried over into our everyday existence.

Mindfulness is especially important to addicts. If we look carefully, we can see the ways in which our addictive behavior patterns distract us from being present with our feelings. Addiction also very often involves plotting various strategies to obtain our "drug" of choice: stealing to support our habit, or manipulating others to get what we want. If we're mindfully centered in the present each moment, we can see the dishonesty and futility of such intrigue, and we will instead focus on enjoying the simple satisfactions of life.

As an aid to this practice, Buddhism offers the FOUR FOUNDATIONS OF MINDFULNESS. Ideally these are to be practiced, not only in meditation, but all the time. The first is CONTEMPLATION OF THE BODY. This can involve simply observing our breath, being mindful of our postures and movements, or being fully aware of our actions at all times. Or it can involve mentally dissecting the body into its various components or elements, down to the smallest detail. We thus become aware that our bodies are actually only collections of thousands of different components.

The Second Foundation of Mindfulness is CONTEMPLATION OF FEELINGS, in which you are aware of what your sense organs perceive and how you're reacting to that sensation. You note if the experience is pleasant, unpleasant, or neutral. If you watch carefully, you'll see that feelings come and go, and you'll avoid becoming attached to them.

The Third Foundation of Mindfulness is CONTEMPLATION OF THE ACTIVITIES OF THE MIND, in which you observe non-judgmentally the moment-by-moment mental processes going on within yourself. For instance if you find yourself getting angry or upset, you simply notice the emotion arise, without identifying with it or pushing it away. You can thus experience your emotions for what they are, and prevent them from ruling you or destroying your serenity.

THE FOURTH NOBLE TRUTH

The Fourth Foundation of Mindfulness is CONTEMPLATION OF PHENOMENA. Here you look with detachment at the objects your mind is focused on. Thus you see the various objects of your mind as they are, free from the exaggerated importance the mind often places on insignificant things. In all these cases the idea is to simply observe what's going on with you right now rather than letting your mind space out into the past, the future, or some place far away.

RIGHT CONCENTRATION is closely related to Right Mindfulness. The word in Pali is SAMADHI, meaning one-pointed concentration in a benevolent state of mind. The idea is to center the mind on one object, letting go of the tendency to obsess over our usual worries and concerns.

Here again we addicts need to discipline our minds. As with most people our minds are like straws in the wind, being buffeted about from thought to thought. Thus it's easy for our addictive nature to take over and control us, leading us to deeper and deeper levels of self-destruction. Through prayer and meditation, as in Step Eleven, we learn to set all that aside and focus our minds so that our addictive nature can't control us anymore.

Many Buddhist teachers encourage students to get in the habit of doing only one thing at a time. That, of course, is directly contradictory to the multi-tasking that has almost become the norm in our modern society. Yet life becomes a lot less stressful when we focus on one task at a time.

THE FOUR NOBLE TRUTHS

Traditionally in Buddhism there are a number of stages in samadhi. Yet for our purposes we might say that all this is a process, and if we apply Right Effort and Right Mindfulness then we can achieve Right Concentration, or one-pointed mind. Another word for Right Concentration is SERENITY, which is also a key component of the recovery process.

The CONTEMPLATIVE components of the Eightfold Path might be considered the portion of the path concerned with prayer and meditation, about which we'll say more later. In general, the Eightfold Path shows us a way to free our minds, think clearly, live an upright and virtuous life, and work for the benefit of all beings.

As an aid to staying on the Eightfold Path, Buddhists take PRECEPTS. These aren't commandments or moral imperatives; rather they're guideposts to help people stay spiritually focused. Some monks and nuns take hundreds of precepts. Almost every different denomination has a slightly different version.

Yet five of the Buddhist Precepts are so valuable in following the Eightfold Path that lay people of all denominations usually take some variation of them. Zen Master Thich Nhat Hanh, head of the Order of Interbeing, calls them "The Five Mindfulness Trainings." His version is so popular that Buddhists from other schools, and even people of other religions, have come to him to study and take the precepts. Here are Thich Nhat Hahn's Five Mindfulness Trainings (1999, pp. 84-96):

1. Aware of the suffering caused by the destruction of life, I am committed to cultivating compassion and learning ways to protect the lives of people, animals, plants, and minerals. I am determined not to kill, not let others kill, and not to support any act of killing in the world, in my thinking, and in my way of life.

2. Aware of the suffering caused by exploitation, social injustice, stealing, and oppression, I am committed to cultivating loving kindness and learning ways to work for the well-being of people, animals, plants, and minerals. I will practice generosity by sharing time, energy and material resources with those who are in real need. I am determined not to steal and not to possess anything that should belong to others. I will respect the property of others, but I will prevent others from profiting from human suffering or the suffering of other species on Earth.

3. Aware of the suffering caused by sexual misconduct, I am committed to cultivating responsibility and learning ways to protect the safety and integrity of individuals, couples, families and society. I am determined not to engage in sexual relations without love and a long-term commitment. To preserve the happiness of myself and others, I am determined to respect my commitments and the commitments of others. I will do everything in my power to protect children from sexual abuse and to prevent couples and families from being broken by sexual misconduct.

4. Aware of the suffering caused by unmindful speech and the inability to listen to others, I am

committed to cultivating loving speech and deep listening in order to bring joy and happiness to others and relieve others of their suffering. Knowing that words can create happiness or suffering, I am determined to learn to speak truthfully, with words that inspire self-confidence, joy and hope. I will not spread news that I do not know to be certain and will not criticize or condemn things of which I am not sure. I will refrain from uttering words that can cause division or discord, or that can cause the family or the community to break. I am determined to make all efforts to reconcile and resolve all conflicts, however small.

5. Aware of the suffering caused by unmindful consumption, I am committed to cultivating good health, both physical and mental, for myself, my family, and my society by practicing mindful eating, drinking, and consuming. I will ingest only items that preserve peace, well-being, and joy in my body, in my consciousness, and in the collective body and consciousness of family and society. I am determined not to use alcohol or any other intoxicant or to ingest foods or other items that contain toxins, such as certain TV programs, magazines, books, films, and conversations. I am aware that to damage my body or my consciousness with these poisons is to betray my ancestors, my parents, my society, and future generations. I will work to transform violence, fear, anger and confusion in myself and in society by practicing a diet for myself and society. I understand that a proper diet is crucial for self-transformation and for the transformation of society.

PART 2: THE TWELVE STEPS

The Twelve-Step movement has a radically different history from that of Buddhism. It's been only about seventy years since William Wilson, or "Bill W," as he came to be called, gave up trying to fight his alcoholism with his own willpower. Bill had studied the writings of Christian mystics, particularly contemporaries like William James and Carl Gustav Jung. Despairing of overcoming his alcoholism by force of willpower, he turned to God for help. The resulting "White Light" spiritual experience convinced him he'd never drink again.

Bill was skillful enough to realize he couldn't recover in isolation. After his awakening, each time he felt like taking a drink he instead called or visited another alcoholic. In time they organized meetings to discuss their alcoholism and share their recovery together. It was awkward at first, but it worked.

Many of the procedures of Alcoholics Anonymous were borrowed from its immediate precursor, the Oxford Group, which was an ecumenical Christian organization designed to help alcoholics. Yet unlike the Oxford Group, A. A. was intended to be nonsectarian rather than Christian. This turned out to be one of its greatest strengths, allowing it to survive long after the Oxford Group had fallen apart.

The A.A. method worked so well that family and friends of alcoholics borrowed the format to create Alanon, Alateen, and Adult Children of

Alcoholics. Then the Twelve-Step method was applied to other addictions: narcotics, marijuana, tobacco, cocaine, and food. Finally arose the groups concerned with the so-called process addictions: gambling, shopping, indebtedness, sex, romance, codependency, and even religion.

In recent years Internet addicts have begun to form groups. There's Emotions Anonymous, for those of us who have trouble handling our feelings. And there are the trauma-oriented groups, for people who have survived everything from incest to head injuries.

Support groups have proliferated so much that the distinction between addicts and so-called "normal" people is becoming increasingly blurred. Despite criticism from certain segments of the mental health community, I think this is a positive development. While A.A. distinguishes alcoholics from social drinkers or "normal" people, if we look closely and understand the all-pervasive nature of addiction we'll see that nearly all of us are addicted to something, even if it's as mundane as watching television incessantly. Indeed our consumer-oriented society seems designed to encourage all of us to get strung out on material possessions.

We've observed that while the Eightfold Path involves eight components that are to be done more or less simultaneously, the Four Noble Truths are sequential. With the Twelve Steps the process is sequential also. We need to do the steps in order, thoroughly understanding and then performing each step in sequence, to get maximum effectiveness from them.

The number twelve is arbitrary. Some recovery groups have added additional steps. But since most groups use the Twelve Steps in some form, for our purposes here we'll stick with the twelve, with some modifications. Rather than adding more steps, I prefer to break some of them down into two or three substeps, which also are best done sequentially. For instance, Step One has two parts; and Step Five has three.

As I mentioned, though it was intended to be nonsectarian A.A borrowed heavily from the Oxford Group. As a result some of the A.A. language has a distinctly Christian flavor to it. Some meetings are still adjourned with the Our Father prayer. Such language critically compromises the stated non-sectarian aim of the movement, and hence needs to be changed. In addition, some of the steps use words like "defects of character" that can encourage guilt feelings in some people.

Some books I've read on recovery accept the A. A. wording of the steps uncritically. Other writers modify the steps so much that they lose some of their original power. I find much of value in the Twelve Steps that I prefer to retain. But in keeping with the intended nondenominational nature of the Twelve Steps, as we go along we'll change the language of some of the steps to make it less Christian-sounding and guilt-inducing.

I'm also changing the tense of these steps from past to present to emphasize that this is an ongoing process, not something we can quickly put behind us, any more than Buddhists may say they have finished with the Four Noble Truths years ago. If you prefer the past-tense wording, feel free to return to that.

I suggest you spend several days or more on each step before going on to the next one, following along in TWELVE STEPS AND TWELVE TRADITIONS or the appropriate guidebook for your particular recovery plan. It's best to keep a journal while working the steps. Each day you can write in your journal concerning the step you're currently working on, being careful to be completely honest with yourself. Thus we begin with Step One, and move through the steps one by one, being sure to complete each step before moving on to the next.

STEP ONE: WE ADMIT THAT, IDENTIFIED WITH OUR EGOTISTICAL "SELVES," WE ARE POWERLESS OVER OUR HUMAN WEAKNESSES; TO THE EXTENT THAT AT TIMES WE'VE BEEN UNABLE TO MANAGE OUR OWN LIVES

Many of us like to think of ourselves as all-powerful. Power, indeed, is an obsession of our contemporary culture, and possibly others as well. Even some religious systems emphasize power. There are all kinds of courses one can take that teach how to gain power over others, as well as over oneself.

In this light, it's revolutionary to state, as the First Step does, that we are powerless over anything. Yet if we look carefully we'll see that every one of us is powerless over something. The exact nature of our powerlessness, or what we're powerless over, varies among us: we may be powerless over alcohol, drugs, food, or sex.

In the First Step for Codependents Anonymous (CODA), we admit we're powerless over other people. In Emotions Anonymous we admit we're powerless over our emotions. Actually all of us are powerless over our emotions, as well as over other people. Some of us just seem to have more of a struggle admitting this powerlessness to ourselves.

If you're a child-abuse survivor, or you're suffering from an incurable disease like AIDS, or you're in recovery from an injury that may limit your ability to lead a normal life, then these are realities over which you're powerless. We can't change the past, be it our own actions or what happened to us.

The issue of powerlessness may be of special concern to those of us who are survivors of abuse. We may have felt powerless most of our lives. And indeed as children we were in fact powerless. We are not responsible for what was done to us.

We ADMIT our powerlessness. We don't boast of it or rejoice in it. After countless failed attempts to reform ourselves through strength of willpower, we've reluctantly come to the conclusion that we're powerless over at least one aspect of our lives.

Yet the first word is "We," not "I." We're able to make this admission about ourselves in the company of others who share a similar weakness or difficulty. Together we admit our powerlessness.

Just as the First Noble Truth reverses popular mythology to warn us that suffering is everywhere and things don't always go according to plan, the First Step helps us overcome our denial of our own powerlessness. In presenting the First Noble Truth the Buddha pointed out several ways in which we are powerless: we may be separated from what we love and forced to live with what we detest; and whether we like it or not we will grow old, become infirm, and die.

The admission that there is any area of our lives over which we are powerless is bound to bring a radical transformation in us. It calls into question the very image of ourselves that we have built up.

If we look carefully we can see that even in the areas where we've been able to change through apparent willpower, the real strength comes not from our egos, but from our higher consciousness. Without that power, we're inevitably ensnared in DUKKHA. Just as we can't control our addictions, neither can we control our birth, our continual aging, our physical limitations, nor our impending disease and death.

Far from enshrining the ego as all-powerful, the Buddha taught that our very notion of having an egotistical self or soul is illusory. We are moment-to-moment constructs that we create, hollow shells without substance. If we look inside our so-called "self" and see that we are ultimately empty, devoid of substance, then it's not at all difficult to realize that we're powerless. THE ROOT OF ALL ADDICTION IS THE FALSE BELIEF IN AN ALL-POWERFUL EGOTISTICAL "SELF" WHICH PRETENDS TO BE IN CONTROL OF ONE'S LIFE.

Most of us have wanted to be powerful at some point in our lives. If we were mistreated as children, or even as adults, we want to be the one in charge so that can't happen to us anymore. Thus many of us try to create a fantasy of ourselves as all-powerful, safe from being hurt again.

From here we may go on to try to play God with the universe as we enshrine our wounded ego. Deep down, we may know it's all a lie. Our addictions and other personal weaknesses show how vulnerable we really are.

Some critics say that admitting our powerlessness discourages people from being rational, thus throwing away one of our best tools. Reason has its place in Buddhism; people are encouraged to test the teachings to see if they correspond to reality. Yet is reason by itself a sound basis for recovery?

The problem is that most addicts are accustomed to rationalizing our actions. In the grip of our addiction we're unable to distinguish this rationalizing from clear thinking. We can give all kinds of reason to ourselves why acting out in our addiction won't hurt this one time.

Let's use anger for an example, since nearly all of us struggle with it. Most of us have seen the evidence, if we look clearly, that anger is destructive to ourselves and our relationships with others. We may truly want to take responsibility for our own anger.

Yet when we get angry, we're likely to tell ourselves that this time is an exception. After all, weren't we being perfectly reasonable just now? The problem is that our partner, the neighbors, or the people in the Middle East are such jerks that any rational person couldn't help getting angry at the way they're acting. And once again we can give all kinds of reasons why we're right and they're wrong.

In Buddhism as in Christianity we're warned to avoid this kind of "logic." We need to calm ourselves, set our "selves" aside, and look at the situation, including our own anger, dispassionately. Some of the language in the Twelve Steps may seem too self-effacing. But the intention is to get our imaginary ego with its fantasy of personal power out of the way so we can see the situation for what it is.

Nor does the Twelve Step system, when properly practiced, encourage the participant to be mindless and irresponsible, as some critics imply. Actually it encourages us to take full responsibility for our actions, even those performed under the spell of addiction; just as in Buddhism one is fully responsible for one's own karmic actions.

The second part of the First Step states that, as a result of our powerlessness, "Our lives have become unmanageable." It's often said that the deeper the crisis into which our addiction or trauma places us, the more dramatic our recovery.

With my compulsive talking, for instance, I am at times powerless; yet thus far it's unclear if it has ever reached the point of making my life unmanageable. Maybe it will, if I see that saying the wrong thing at the wrong time damages my professional life, as well as my personal relationships. Otherwise I could remain a compulsive talker until I die. I may control it for a time; but in unmindful moments it may return.

On the other hand, at several points in the past my compulsive sexual acting out, despite numerous resolutions to the contrary, definitely made my life unmanageable. Now after eight years of attending twelve-step meetings I no longer feel tempted to act out as I used to. It's these kinds of life-threatening, self-destructive behavior patterns that are most suited to the Twelve-Step process. Sometimes it's only when we see how we're destroying ourselves that we can find the courage and humility to admit our powerlessness over our lives.

To the extent that we base our lives on the delusion of personal power, our lives are likely to appear unmanageable. We can find peace only when we acknowledge our true nature by admitting that our egotistical "self" can't control our lives. Now the question becomes, if we can't control our own lives, who can? This brings us to Step Two.

STEP TWO: WE BECOME AWARE OF A CONSCIOUSNESS FAR GREATER THAN OUR EGOTISTICAL "SELVES" THAT CAN RESTORE US TO WHOLENESS

Rather than blindly believing what we're taught, the Buddha encouraged his followers to question and examine his teachings, as well as those of other teachers, to see what our experience shows us to be true. Though in its original form Step Two uses the word "belief", I think this is the kind of faith we're talking about here.

In part this conviction comes from deep intuition. But equally importantly it comes from our experience, and from our observations of others in recovery. This shows the value of attending meetings where we listen to testimonials from people who have recovered from weaknesses similar to our own. As we observe how others have been healed by allowing a consciousness greater than their "selves" to guide them, we begin to believe it will work for us also.

Of course we can offer all kinds of reasons why our situation is unique. Yet even when some of those arguments may be valid, we still can perceive parallels between our lives and those of others if we keep our minds open. As we see, beyond the obvious differences in lifestyle, the similarities between our lives and theirs, we begin to feel less isolated and alone in the universe.

Does Step Two contradict the Buddhist principle of taking responsibility for yourself, to

"Be lamps unto yourselves"? Actually the very notion of admitting our own powerlessness over one area of our life, and then becoming convinced that a Higher Consciousness can help us, is a way of taking responsibility.

I once heard someone ask a monk, "Do Buddhists believe in God?" The monk replied, "What is God?" I doubt if any Buddhists believe in a judgmental Father figure who punishes evildoers for all eternity. Yet all religions, including Buddhism, seem to acknowledge the presence of a Consciousness greater than our so-called "selves."

Buddhism is sometimes seen as an "atheistic" philosophy that makes each individual responsible for herself or himself. Compared with some other religions, Buddhism does emphasize individual initiative in seeking truth, as well as personal responsibility for our actions.

Yet in all forms of Buddhism there are the Three Treasures, the Buddha, Dharma, and Sangha, to which Buddhists pray daily when we take refuge. These can be perceived as Consciousness greater than our individual ego, which we've already noted is powerless. Indeed, as we've seen, Buddhism teaches that the very notion of this ego is an illusion.

I'm replacing the term "Higher Power" with "Higher Consciousness" to avoid misunderstanding. Admitting the existence of a power greater than our "selves" can cause problems with people raised in Judaeo-Christian-Islamic religions, since we've been taught to believe that the patriarchal god of these religions is the only true Higher Power in the

universe. The use of the term "Higher Consciousness" here is designed to open our awareness to a
Divine Presence that is much broader than that. We
thus recognize that there exists Consciousness in the
universe that transcends our individual egos.

This could refer to a personal deity; but it's
not necessarily limited to that. We could just as well
call it the Buddha-Nature. The Buddha, Dharma,
and Sangha are three examples of this Higher
Consciousness; nearly all Buddhists pray to these
when we take refuge.

In addition, in all forms of Mahayana
Buddhism there are celestial Buddhas and
Bodhisattvas: Amitabha, Avalokiteshvara, Guanyin,
Tara, Manjushri, and many others. Although none
of these celestial beings are omnipotent, people
revere them and pray to them daily. Any of these
deities can be regarded as a Consciousness greater
than our "selves."

Almost half of all Buddhist deities are
goddesses; and none can be confused with the
sometimes judgmental patriarchal god of Judaism,
Christianity, and Islam. Even in these religions, it
has been argued, the image of an angry, shaming,
patriarchal god may be a misinterpretation of
scripture. In any case, it's important to see our
Higher Consciousness not as a judgmental father
figure but as a compassionate ally who works with
us to free us from our addictive habits.

At the other extreme, there's always a
temptation to try to use our Higher Consciousness
to satisfy our cravings. If we do the steps correctly

we won't make that error. We turn to our Higher Consciousness after we've realized that our egotistical will is incapable of running our lives in a sane, constructive manner.

No traditional form of Buddhism teaches us to regard our egotistical "self" as supreme; rather we are brought to the understanding that this "self" upon which we've depended is unsteady, ever-changing, and hence undependable. The restoration that Steps One and Two offer us means letting go of the delusion that we are or have an omnipotent "ego" that can do whatever it chooses. Once that delusion is gone, we can open up to the healing energy that is there for all of us.

Steps One and Two correspond to Right Understanding, the first part of the Eightfold Path. We need to correct our distorted view of ourselves and the world before we can act intelligently. If we cultivate the awareness of our Buddha Nature, we have an invincible ally in our effort to overcome our addiction.

Our own unsteady willpower doesn't work for us because it's based on the delusion that we each exist as self-sufficient entities with our own power. We need to let go of that delusion and open our awareness to the Buddha Nature. When you finally feel you are ready to open yourself completely to that Consciousness, then it's time to move on to Step Three.

STEP THREE: WE MAKE A DECISION TO RETURN OUR LIVES AND OUR WILL TO THE CARE OF THIS CONSCIOUSNESS GREATER THAN OUR "SELVES," AS BEST WE UNDERSTAND THIS CONSCIOUSNESS

This step begins with a decision. This is like the Second component of the Eightfold Path: having understood the true nature of reality, we set our goals accordingly. If we decide in Step Three to turn our lives and our will over to our Higher Consciousness, who has been running our lives until now?

If we look carefully, we'll see that we've been effectively out of control all our lives, until we return our life and will back to our Buddha Nature. Really, our Higher Consciousness has been in charge all along. Only our pretence that our ego has any power has caused the chaos in our lives: self-will run riot. The decision we make in Step Three is to let go of our delusion of an all-powerful, egotistical "self," and let the real power in the Universe guide us from now on without obstruction on the part of our imaginary ego.

Originally Step Three was written, "Made a decision to turn our lives and our will over to the care of God as we understood Him." The use of the masculine pronoun presents problems for some Mahayana Buddhists, as well as people of other faiths, since some of us may visualize God as a feminine deity like Gwanyin, or possibly even an impersonal Divine force. Fortunately many

63

programs have rewritten the words to remedy this. Buddhists can advise others to also make this revision: "God as we understood God;" or better yet, "This Consciousness greater than ourselves, as best we understand this Consciousness."

Since the word "God" may have negative connotations to some, it might be advisable to substitute "Higher Consciousness" for the word "God." Buddhists and others who don't have a patriarchal conception of God can thus become instrumental in widening the scope of the Twelve Steps to appeal to people who might otherwise be turned off by the wording of the Steps. Twelve Step meetings need to be inclusive of people from all religions; and the language needs to accommodate that diversity.

Step Three is a crucial threshold in the recovery process. It's the point at which, having let go of the delusion that we're in control of all areas of our lives, we restore our will to the Divine Consciousness, the only source of our strength. What we're doing in Step Three is to give ourselves over to the Dharma, our Higher Awareness, so that from now on our entire lives will revolve around that Consciousness.

We may have done this in the past with another human being whom we tried to make into our Higher Power. If so, we've seen the disastrous results such worship of another human being usually creates in our lives. Now we will do this with the one Power in the universe to whom we can safely give up control.

STEP THREE

Once while working either Step Three or Step Eleven I told my sponsor I couldn't do it right because "I really don't understand God." Quite an admission for someone with a Master of Divinity degree, isn't it? But at the time I felt that the mysteries of the Divine overwhelmed me. My sponsor assured me that I don't have to claim any special knowledge of God to work these steps. I only need to do my best to seek God as best I understand Her.

I've observed at times that when my Higher Consciousness suggests something, even if it's an off-the-wall idea that I'd never thought of before, on some deep level it ultimately makes sense. On the other hand, if an inner voice suggests something destructive, like taking harmful drugs, killing myself, or hurting someone, I know that's not my Higher Consciousness talking at all.

The kind of reasoning my Higher Consciousness offers feels entirely different from the rationalizing my addict has used to try to justify my acting out. If I listen carefully to my Higher Consciousness, I can see that it's the only valid source for reasonable thought. And I need Her reasoning power to take a dispassionate look at what I've been doing to myself and others. Then, with my Higher Consciousness now in charge of my life, I can see clearly what I have done, what the result has been for me and others, and what to do next.

The Buddhist threefold Refuge Prayer, "I take refuge in the Buddha, I take refuge in the Dharma, I take refuge in the Sangha," is a way of doing Step Three. Even for Theravada Buddhists who don't recognize personal deities, the Buddha, Dharma and Sangha are higher states of awareness to which one turns over one's life by taking refuge in them. Actually, as Thich Nhat Hanh explains, the prayer is repetitive; since the Three Treasures are really one, and to take refuge in one is to take refuge in all three.

Incidentally, while taking refuge in the Buddha, Dharma, and Sangha is usually thought to constitute becoming a Buddhist, it doesn't preclude participation in other religions. Many people have taken refuge as Buddhists while continuing their previous religions. Buddhist was never meant to be an exclusive religion.

For that matter, taking refuge in God or Christ can be just as valid. What's important is to understand that your salvation lies in your Higher Consciousness as best you understand Her or Him, not in your egotistical self-will. With that in mind, it's time to take a careful look at this "self" you've imagined yourself to be.

STEP FOUR: WE HONESTLY AND PAINSTAKINGLY EXAMINE OURSELVES AS WE REALLY ARE, SPARING NO DETAIL, HOWEVER EMBARASSING

Most programs speak of a "moral inventory." Some people in recovery, including me, are fine with that phrase. However I've observed that the word "moral" pushes even more people's buttons than the word "God." It brings up the whole notion of judgment, even if unintentionally so.

There've been estimates that for every addict who's helped, there may be two others who are so turned off by words like "moral inventory" that they go elsewhere, either finding another route to recovery or eventually destroying themselves through their addiction. While ethics are essential to Buddhism, I'd like to avoid this misunderstanding by deleting the word "moral" from this step.

People of all faiths can benefit from Twelve-Step meetings that use language that's non-patriarchal, guilt-free, and non-shaming. We don't want to encourage feelings of being different—with implied moral inferiority—from the general population. It's a middle path we seek, taking responsibility for our actions without laying guilt trips on ourselves.

As we've noted above, our problem as addicts is not that we're morally inferior, but that, like everyone else, we've deluded ourselves into believing in our "selves" as separate, egotistical entities. Having given our lives over to our Higher Consciousness in Step Three, we're now ready look at ourselves dispassionately.

Still, it's important that our self-examination be honest and painstaking. I won't say "fearless," because this could be a scary experience for some of us; yet it will help our recovery greatly if we cast our fears aside to follow through with it carefully and completely. That, I believe, is most likely the intent of the word "fearless." In other words, you want to take your time and carefully look at your life and your behavior patterns to see what your true motivations have been.

This isn't an exercise in self-condemnation; for you may note your good points as well as your weaknesses. More accurately, you will record what you see in yourself without at this point judging what is "good" and what's "bad." Getting beyond those kinds of moral judgments helps you discern what your true values have been, based on your patterns of behavior.

In doing your Fourth Step you may see an opportunity to detach yourself from your "self," almost as if observing another person. The idea is to avoid being defensive about your mistakes. If you're totally honest, yet comfortably detached, you'll be able to evaluate yourself objectively, realizing once again that this "self" you thought was running your life is illusory and has no power. Thus you need feel neither pride nor shame in evaluating what you have done. Completing the process helps you to let go of those emotions and the false self-concept that has spawned them.

Since this examination can best be done in writing, Step Four again points out the importance of keeping a journal. I find it best to work on it over a period of days or even weeks, each day adding new insights about myself as they occur to me.

Since in Step Three I've turned my life and will over to my Higher Consciousness, I find it helpful to listen to this Consciousness as I write down my inventory, to see if there are aspects of myself I may have left out. Sometimes this even grows into a dialogue; as though my lower and Higher "selves" are discussing my various character traits.

The word "painstaking," like the phrase "searching and fearless" implies that you're to leave no stone upturned in seeking out your own true nature, and that you must not stop short of admitting painful, difficult, even fearsome truths about yourself. Look carefully at the role of emotions like fear, anger, and guilt in your life. You may find it especially helpful here to work with a mentor or sponsor; or else to participate in a Fourth-Step workshop with others in recovery.

When a retail operation does an inventory, they must be careful to list all merchandise, from best-selling items to worthless stuff that's just taking up valuable floor space. That's how you need to do your personal self-examination: searching your deepest personal closets, attics, and cellars to see what's really there in your life. It may seem like a chore, but before you're through you may feel delight at the treasures you've found in the back room.

Having taken a good look at yourself, and then recorded what you see, it's time to sort the stuff and throw out what you don't want to keep. To do that you must first select your least desirable habits, the ones you least like to admit and most need to change, and confess fully how you've acted. That brings us to Step Five.

STEP FIVE: WE ADMIT TO OUR HIGHER CONSCIOUSNESS, TO OURSELVES, AND TO ANOTHER SAFE AND SYMPATHETIC HUMAN BEING THE EXACT NATURE OF OUR PERSONAL WEAKNESSES

One of the purposes of working the steps is to overcome the guilt and shame we feel. Only if we allow ourselves to come to terms with these feelings will we be in a position to let go of them. Most of us have done things we aren't proud of.

We need to honestly acknowledge what we've done that we don't feel good about, and then let it go. Of course we'll want to mention our good points too, but the main focus now is on our errors. No matter what we've done, with the aid of our Higher Consciousness we can fully atone for these mistakes, change our ways, and move on.

Here again the traditional language, "the exact nature of our wrongs," may alienate some people. We addicts need to get beyond our feelings of guilt and shame, not wallow in them. This is especially important to those of us who are survivors of child abuse. We must learn to stop blaming ourselves for the abuse we suffered and the trauma that has resulted in our lives.

Yet only the very last word is a problem here. If we've done things to ourselves and others that have compromised our own ethical standards, then it's time for us to acknowledge this fact—so long as we remember that we've done so under the grip of addiction or delusion.

While you're confessing your own misdeeds, should you also mention the wrongs that have been done to you? Certainly if you're a child-abuse survivor you might want to do that. Sometimes it's easier to admit your own mistakes if you also note the ways in which others have mistreated you.

For instance, when I do my Fifth Step I often begin by listing the ways I've been mistreated as a child and an adult. Then I go on from there to admit that I have mistreated myself perhaps worse than anyone else has mistreated me, and that some of that has carried over into my mistreatment of others. Thus it helps to show how my personal flaws were shaped in reaction to treatment by others.

But I must not use this as an excuse to justify my own mistreatment of others. Especially I must not pretend that I can't help being as dysfunctional as I've been, as though I can't change. I CAN change; and admitting my own weaknesses is a step toward changing them. Step Five can be a greatly cleansing and freeing experience, helping us to overcome the guilt and shame we all have felt about our addictions.

There are three parts to this step, and I prefer to take them in sequence. For me the first part is the easiest. I note that my Higher Consciousness never seems interested in judging or condemning me, but rather in helping me see my true nature so I can act accordingly. Thus Step Five is in a way a continuation of Step Four. What's new is that now

I focus on the parts of myself I dislike, and confess them to my Higher Consciousness, knowing that She has already forgiven me, as Her true nature is compassion.

Confession and repentance play a vital role in Buddhism, as in many other religions, and Step Five is a wonderful opportunity to practice this. Many Buddhist sanghas have prayers of repentance that are recited on the full moon every month. If you can attend such a ceremony it will help intensify the experience, whether or not you're a Buddhist. These monthly prayers of repentance are particularly effective if performed in conjunction with the Fifth Step. Other religions, including Christianity, offer comparable ceremonies.

In the second part of Step Five I return to myself, noting that even this notion of my having a "self" is an artificial construct. Having confessed my errors to my Higher Consciousness, and knowing that She has already forgiven me, I now admit to myself all my own weaknesses and transgressions, asking that I forgive myself as my Higher Consciousness has forgiven me. This part could take a little longer.

Don't presume you've already completed this in Step Four. Do several days or more of journal work on this, being as honest and forgiving toward yourself as you can.

Like most people I find the third part of Step Five the most challenging. I try to find someone else who is also in a recovery program, and who seems understanding and compassionate and willing to listen. There must be no hidden agenda between us. A potential business client is out of the question, as is someone to whom I feel sexually attracted or who seems sexually or romantically interested in me.

Since people are short on time, I sometimes offer to reciprocate by listening to the other person's Fifth Step after or before he or she listens to mine. I find it essential, though, to do this sequentially, rather than let it break down into random conversation. One of us listens while the other talks, and then we reverse roles at an agreed-on time. It's important to be thorough, and to stay focused on the business at hand.

This can also help in locating a sponsor or mentor if you're looking for one. If the third part of the Fifth Step works out well you may suggest it as an ongoing relationship. Most people find the process of serving as a sponsor to another person in a recovery program is very helpful to their own recovery.

Yet the guidelines I've suggested for doing a Fifth Step with someone are even more important regarding sponsorship. It's especially important that there be no sexual attraction either way.

When it's done correctly, all your Step work seems to proceed more efficiently when you're working with a sponsor. There's a great relief when you admit your most embarrassing secrets to another human being, if you've chosen that other person carefully. Oftentimes we find that the self-disclosure that we initially feel so much shame about may not seem shameful at all to the other person, especially if he or she has secrets also.

Besides, by admitting these shameful secrets of yours, you acknowledge that the "self" you've presented to the world is a lie. The sooner you open up and admit you're not who you've pretended to be, the sooner you become ready to allow your Higher Consciousness to change you. That brings us to Step Six.

STEP SIX: WE BECOME ENTIRELY READY TO ALLOW OUR HIGHER CONSCIOUSNESS TO WORK WITH US TO TRANSFORM ALL OUR PERSONAL WEAKNESSES INTO STRENGTHS

In the traditional version, we "were entirely ready to have God remove these defects of character." Here again, we may want to change the wording somewhat, as these words can be troubling to some people in recovery. Let's consider why Step Six is worded the way it is.

Of all the world's religions, to my knowledge only certain forms of Christianity teach that humans are basically sinful, incapable of doing good on our own. Even within Christianity there have been movements and denominations that have sprung up in rejection of this doctrine of original sin.

Unfortunately the founders of the Oxford Group, and to a certain extent of AA itself, had their roots in the traditional, sin-obsessed form of Christianity; and this mentality is reflected in places in AA literature. As several critics have pointed out, the references to "moral inventory," "wrongs," and "defects of character" reinforce the image of the addict as morally inferior to so-called "normal" people, and thus encourage feelings of guilt and shame. As we've already noted, this distinction between "addicts" and "normal people" is bogus, as virtually everyone suffers from an addiction to something.

The notion of ourselves as sinners reinforces our sense of unworthiness. And then God seems like a deus ex machina coming to rescue us from our own sinful nature. We are, as critics have noted, seen simultaneously as helpless yet morally culpable.

Hence the traditional phrase, "defects of character" undoubtedly pushes some people's buttons, possibly to the extent of driving people away from the recovery movement altogether. I'm offering "personal weaknesses" as a possible substitute. I suggest you find wording that inspires you to work with your Higher Consciousness to overcome the weaknesses that have crippled you until now.

It may seem that these personal weaknesses result from our addictions; but more likely it's the other way around. Our personal weaknesses result from our illusory image of ourselves as self-sufficient entities, playing god with the universe. That's what we need to do in Step Six: look at the false image we've created of ourselves so we can let go of it.

In reality the only true Self you or I have is our Buddha Nature, our Higher Consciousness. In that Buddha Nature there is no defect, however much we may have let our delusions—and our addictions—misdirect our lives.

If your real Self isn't defective, why have you been stuck in all these dysfunctional behavior patterns? It's because you've denied your true Self, which is simply a manifestation of your Higher

Consciousness, and propped up your false egotistical self-conception. Once you realize who "you" really are, the need for such self-rationalization disappears, and you become ready to reaffirm your true nature. This means that you need to trust your Higher Consciousness completely.

But as we've noted, it isn't only you and I who are dysfunctional. The whole universe is enmeshed in DUKKHA. Why doesn't our Higher Consciousness fix it?

Different religions handle the problem of evil a bit differently, though it may amount to the same thing in the end. In Buddhist teaching, suffering comes from karmic actions based on hate, greed, and delusion. None of the Buddhist deities created the universe the way it is; and none of them are omnipotent. Things just are the way they are, and not even God can change that.

Regardless of how you picture your Higher Consciousness, you might see Him or Her or It not as an all-powerful ruler, but as a loving senior partner in this endeavor. Our Higher Power can't change the karmic laws of the universe, but S/He is always there for us. In fact, your Higher Consciousness is your Buddha Nature, your only true Self.

As you may have noticed by now, from Step Two on the steps come in pairs. The even numbered steps prepare us, and then with the next odd-numbered step we boldly move on. Thus Step Two prepares us to turn to our Higher

78

Consciousness, and with Step Three we actually acknowledge our Higher Consciousness's rule over our life. In Step Four we list our weaknesses as well as our strengths; and then in Step Five we confess our weaknesses three times. In Step Six we prepare ourselves to let go of our weaknesses, along with our illusory self-conception that has until now fed them. Now, in Step Seven we will actually let our Higher Consciousness work with us to transform our weaknesses into strengths.

STEP SEVEN: WE WHOLEHEARTEDLY INVITE OUR HIGHER CONSCIOUSNESS TO WORK WITH US TO TRANSFORM ALL OF OUR PERSONAL WEAKNESSES INTO STRENGTHS

The traditional wording states, "Humbly asked Him to remove our shortcomings." As with Step Three, this patriarchal reference to God as "Him" has already been changed in many programs. That's consistent with the intended non-denominational orientation of the Twelve Step movement. In addition, I've made a few cosmetic changes to emphasize, as in Step Six, that this is a process involving a cooperative partnership between the "I" that I think I am and my Higher Consciousness.

Why "transform," rather than "remove"? When I'm working the steps, sometimes I arrive at Steps Eight, Nine, or Ten, only to notice I still have the same faults I had before. At this point in my journal I then turn to my Higher Power and complain, "God you were supposed to have removed all my character defects back in Step Seven." My Higher Power then reminds me that even with Her help it will take years to transform dysfunctional habits that I've spent decades of my life acquiring.

The traditional wording of Step Seven almost gives the picture of God reaching into your interior to surgically remove all your defects. If only it were that simple! Old habit patterns aren't that easily changed. You begin the transformation when you decide to let go of your egotistical self-conception and let your Higher Consciousness transform you.

Still, it's important to remember here that we're asking our Higher Consciousness to help us transform all of our weaknesses, not just some of our own choosing. We need to let go of our limited view of ourselves and prepare to travel the road to perfection. We may never actually get there, at least not in this life; but we can go ahead and embark on the journey.

I'm replacing "humbly" with "whole-heartedly." Some feminist writers insist that women and other oppressed people need to learn self-esteem more than humility. That may be true; though I don't think the two are really contradictory. I suspect nearly all of us, whatever our social station, may suffer from feelings of inadequacy. And all of us need help with these and other weaknesses. Admitting that need requires humility.

Here again, we're reminded that the shortcomings or weaknesses we perceive in our "selves" are invariably the result of our false view of ourselves as separate entities. By working with our Higher Consciousness we stop clinging to our self-image and begin to experience oneness with that Consciousness. The qualities of compassion and humility that we're nurturing in ourselves are diametrically opposed not only to egotism, self-centeredness, and attempts to control others, but equally to codependence, passive-aggressiveness, and self-victimization.

I find the personal deities in the Mahayana forms of Buddhism especially helpful in healing from addiction. Many Mahayana Buddhists feel drawn to a particular Bodhisattva in a relationship that may reach beyond one's present lifespan.

In the tantric forms of Mahayana like Vajrayana or Shingon there are elaborate visualization techniques that assist the student in his or her transformation. It's said that some of these tantric techniques can be helpful in more rapidly overcoming addiction. However they require advanced study with a realized Master; otherwise they can be misused. Hence I can't discuss them effectively here.

As your self-image transforms under the influence of your Higher Consciousness, your ego-based weaknesses give way of their own accord. You begin to see that there's no reason to be self-centered anymore, as the "self" that has tried to center the universe around it is an illusion. Thus your Higher Consciousness does indeed begin to help you overcome your perceived shortcomings.

Of course this will take time. Step Seven, like the other steps, is a process that continues more or less indefinitely. But as you let go of your false conception of your "self" as a being with permanent strengths and weaknesses, your dysfunctional behavior patterns will be thus transformed into effective actions that will benefit not only you, but other beings as well.

STEP SEVEN

Now comes the hard part. Because we have deluded ourselves into thinking we were separate entities, and at times we've allowed our addictions to run our lives, most of us have done things that we're not proud of. Now that we've gotten our egos out of the way and looked at ourselves dispassionately, it's time for us to note these unhealthy past actions of ours and think about making amends as appropriate.

STEP EIGHT: WE MAKE A LIST OF ALL THE PERSONS WHOM WE HAVE HARMED IN OUR LIVES, INCLUDING OURSELVES, MOST LIKELY; AND WE BECOME WILLING TO MAKE AMENDS TO THEM ALL. WE ALSO LIST ALL THOSE WHO HAVE HARMED US, AND WE CONSIDER WHAT IT WOULD TAKE FOR US TO FORGIVE THEM COMPLETELY

Fortunately the Eighth Step doesn't ask us to list everyone we've ever insulted, offended, or been unfair to. If it did, the list might seem endless. Instead we're merely asked to list those whom we have harmed in some way.

For most of us, we need to include ourselves on the list; for whom have we hurt more than ourselves? Some of us would long ago have stopped seeing a friend who treated us as badly as we have ourselves. We may also include parents, siblings, business partners, friends, ex-friends, lovers, and ex-lovers: those whom we have cheated, abused, or taken advantage of. For some people it may be a long list. Yet it's important to be thorough, as it is with all the steps.

An obvious question might be, "Since the past is over and done with, why not just forget it and move on?" Yes, that's precisely our goal here. But if we remember how we've mistreated other people in the grip of our addiction, we most likely still have guilt feelings about what we've done.

Making amends is the surest way to release this guilt.

Though Buddhism emphasizes living in the present, it also notes that the karma from our previous actions will have consequences in the future. Many people in recovery find that after they've completed Step Eight they're much less likely to mistreat others. By looking at how your past actions have injured yourself and others, you give yourself the opportunity to make sure you act more wisely from now on. It also helps you overcome the notion that you exist as a separate entity with no consequences of your actions for others.

I've added to this step that we should also note those who have harmed us. We need to forgive them; but we can't do that until we've noted just how they harmed us. This is one of the best ideas presented in Charlotte Kasl's book, MANY ROADS, ONE JOURNEY: MOVING BEYOND THE TWELVE STEPS.

For abuse survivors this may be the most important part of this step. We need to stop feeling guilty or responsible for what others have done to us, especially when we were little. If we've been hurt by others, we need to acknowledge this fact, for undoubtedly it affects us even now, however long ago it happened.

It's important, though, not to maintain a grudge list of all the people who have messed us over, and all the things they've done to us. The purpose of listing our past abusers is to understand what happened, how it's affected us, and how important it is for us to let go of it and move on. Besides, we mustn't let this detract from our equally important task of remembering what we have done to ourselves and others, for which we need to take responsibility.

If you try to excuse your mistreatment of others on the basis that you yourself were previously abused, that will get you nowhere. Your abusers could just as easily justify their abuse of you in the same way, since they undoubtedly were themselves survivors of abuse. It's often the case that people who have been abused themselves later go on to abuse others.

Thus it's essential for each of us to take responsibility for our own actions, even while noting that we were misguided because we ourselves were abused. Only then can we be free from our compulsive behavior patterns that cause us to mistreat ourselves and others. In this way we can break the cycle of abuse and stop creating negative karma.

One other little amendment I sometimes add to Step Eight is to consider the various sub-personalities that make up the fictitious creation I call my "self": the adult, the little boy, the teenage girl, the young adult, and so forth. In what ways have these various characters abused and mistreated each other, and what can each abuser do to atone for his or her abusive behavior? I find this internal dynamic an especially important aspect of Step

Eight, and I try to work with it each time I do this step.

Despite what some people might think, being in touch with the various sub-personalities within ourselves is not psychosis. You need to let go of the notion that you're a consistent, self-sufficient personality with unchanging features. Not only are you not the same person "you" were thirty years ago; but even on a moment to moment basis your feelings change.

"You" are a process; and these sub-personalities are just as real, if not more so, as the "person" you go around pretending to be. Getting in touch with these different aspects of yourself helps you to give up this false self-image and observe what's really going on with you. In some cases the process of forgiving yourself for what you've done to hurt yourself could be one of the most important aspects of Steps Eight and Nine.

STEP NINE: WHEN POSSIBLE WE TRY TO MAKE DIRECT AMENDS TO PEOPLE WHOM WE HAVE HARMED (INCLUDING OURSELVES), EXCEPT WHEN TO DO SO COULD INJURE THEM, OURSELVES, OR OTHERS. IN ADDITION, WE MAKE A CONSCIENTIOUS EFFORT TO FORGIVE THOSE WHO HAVE HARMED US.

Having acknowledged the wrongs done to us by others, and the wrongs we have done to ourselves and others, we now proceed to set things right, as best we can. Making amends to those we've hurt is important, frightening as it may seem. It doesn't mean groveling or begging or putting ourselves down; it means simply acknowledging what we've done, apologizing, and resolving not to repeat the mistake. It could be a simple expression of regret in some cases; in other instances it could mean paying back money we stole to support our habit.

Most guidebooks encourage us to make amends in person when possible. That's a good idea if you can actually meet with the person; but what if it's someone who lives a thousand miles away? You don't need to wait three years until you again see the person you've harmed. A letter, E-mail message, or possibly even a phone call will work. I'm placing those in preferential order. You want to think carefully about what you're going to say, so a phone call might be less desirable here.

What if this is someone with whom you're out of touch, or avoiding for good reason? Step Nine is wise in warning us not to further muddy the waters. The spouse of the person with whom you committed adultery may not really need to know about the hurt you caused—provided that you carefully avoid further transgressions. You could even place yourself or someone else in danger by confessing your transgressions to the wrong person.

Sometimes the best way to make amends is to repent and change our behavior completely, so as to become loving, giving, open, ethical, and non-devious from now on. Since our Higher Consciousness is now in charge of our life, with Her or His help that should be possible regardless of what we've done wrong in the past. The best way to make amends is often to quietly turn over a new leaf in our lives, and make it permanent and consistent.

In Buddhism as in Christianity there's much emphasis on repentance. Traditional religions emphasize this because it's a way of overcoming the enormous burden of karma we've accumulated in this and perhaps previous lives. We do this by atoning for some of the damage we've caused. The Ninth Step offers a systematic avenue by which we can accomplish this.

Buddhist sutras say Buddha converted Angulimala, a vicious serial killer, and persuaded him to become a monk to atone for his murders. It's said that Angulimala became the gentlest of mendicants, not even trying to defend himself against villagers who attacked and beat him for his past crimes. No one is beyond redemption.

I usually begin my Ninth Step by writing a letter to myself, apologizing for all the ways in which I have hurtfully mistreated myself, been untrue to myself, or abused myself. Asking myself for forgiveness, I promise to do better in the future. Once I've made amends to myself, it becomes easier to make amends to other people.

Here again I've added the part about forgiving those who have wronged us. Forgiveness does not mean denying what they did to you. It means acknowledging what happened to you, and then letting it go. It does you no good to hold grudges all your life; that would be like living with a slow-acting poison. You've carried that burden long enough; let's put it down now.

Should you contact those who have abused you to tell them you forgive them? If that will help you forgive them, then fine. But you can't force or even persuade your abusers to make amends to you; that's their decision. If there's any chance that re-contacting a past abuser will place you in danger of being abused again in any way, you must not do it.

Also, if you take the moral high ground and tell a past abuser how evil he or she has been, "But I forgive you!" the person may well get defensive. You need to look carefully at your own motivation: are you really interested in having a healthier relationship with this person, or do you just want to create guilt in the other person for what he or she did to you? You mustn't contact the person until you're sure you really want to forgive him or her completely. In addition, be sure it's totally safe for both of you and it's likely to help you relate better in the future. In some cases it's best to do the work of forgiveness by yourself.

Spiritual leaders throughout history have offered some powerful role models in forgiveness. Buddha consistently forgave those who attacked or reviled him. Jesus was equally compassionate in praying for his own killers.

In our present era, His Holiness the Dalai Lama of Tibet is said to pray daily for the Chinese rulers who have occupied his native country, driven him into exile, slandered him repeatedly, purposely undermined the Tibetan religion and culture, and intimidated any nation that seeks to recognize his government in exile. Buddhism teaches that people who commit such vicious crimes will face terrible agony in the future for what they've done. Hence His Holiness feels great compassion for what the Chinese rulers are doing to themselves. Besides, on a daily level the prayers of His Holiness keep him loving and compassionate rather than vengeful. You and I could hardly ask for a better role model.

Having done the work of reconciliation and forgiveness, now it's time to take another look at this "self" you've imagined yourself to be. That brings us to Step Ten.

STEP TEN: WE CONTINUE TO BE MIND-FULLY AWARE OF ALL OUR MOTIVES AND ACTIONS. WHEN WE MAKE A MISTAKE, WE PROMPTLY ADMIT IT AND RESOLVE TO DO BETTER FROM NOW ON. AT THE SAME TIME, WE ACCEPT OURSELVES FULLY AND REAFFIRM OUR BASIC WORTH AS HUMAN BEINGS.

The purpose of Step Ten is to look at yourself as honestly and objectively as you can, so that you can monitor your own progress effectively. The more dispassionate you can be while doing this, the more effectively you'll be able to evaluate yourself. Likewise the self-evaluation can help you learn to be detached from your "self," not emotionally caught up in your own head-games. As many a philosopher has wisely stated, there is no more valuable gift than to truly understand oneself.

It's important to keep on doing this, as there's still a temptation to slip back into our egos at any time. The whole world around us seems based on egotism and competition, and at any moment we may fear that we'll be swallowed up. We need to keep reminding ourselves that this egotistic self-nature is a delusion that we have already offered up to our Buddha Nature or Higher Consciousness.

The second part of Step Ten says, "When we make a mistake, we promptly admit it." We're human; we all make mistakes. Rather than clinging to our false pride and defending what we've done, we open ourselves up and admit our failings.

Some people claim there are no mistakes, since life is an ongoing learning process. It's true that whatever we do and whatever happens to us can be a lesson in learning how to do better. Still, I think it's okay to regret something we have or haven't done, provided we don't get hung up emotionally on the regret. Rather we can use the experience to find a way to make our lives work better from now on.

In my case, for example, I can't help regretting the two times in the past two years that I've lost my wallet with all my identification, cash, and other valuables. The incidents have helped me admit I need to practice mindfulness, and possibly could use professional help with my Attention Deficit Disorder. But in all honesty I'd have to say I've wished I'd been more mindful at the time, given the loss and inconvenience.

Once again, the first person to whom you need to admit your errors is yourself. Being honest with yourself is the foundation for honesty with others. Once you've been completely honest with yourself then you'll feel more able to open up to others as appropriate.

As most recovery guidebooks note, "slips" are almost inevitable for most of us. We temporarily lose touch with our Higher Consciousness, and then we fall back into our false sense of "self." We may try to convince ourselves that it's safe for us to act out now, as we're beyond temptation. Then the next thing we know we're back in our former destructive patterns.

When this happens to you, be careful not to rationalize what you've done. At the same time, though, don't get caught up in guilt or shame. If you feel bad about yourself you're more likely to continue acting out, and you could possibly lose your recovery altogether.

Most recovering addicts have slips, so you're not alone if you have one. Just resume your step-work, going back to Step One if you need to. Return your life to your Higher Consciousness, and then continue as before.

When you go to your recovery meeting, talk dispassionately about your slip, admitting what you've done without shaming yourself or putting yourself down before the group. If it's a supportive meeting people won't judge you. If they do you need to find another meeting as soon as you can. Other people have slips too, so no one has any reason to look down on you.

The third part here is one I feel it's valuable to add. We want to acknowledge our successes as well as our failures, and our basic self-worth as much as our shortcomings. Many of us in recovery are struggling with negative self-images that we need to get beyond.

When people talk about "low self-esteem," they seem to be talking about these feelings of inadequacy. Usually this means you have unmet expectations of what you ought to be like. I don't think it necessarily solves the problem to merely try to develop a more positive self-image; that may only set you up for more feelings of failure. If you try to replace your negative self-image with a positive one you may still end up feeling self-absorbed, and very likely self-critical.

You may think you have a weak or strong ego. You may have positive or negative feelings about yourself. In either case, though, you're obsessed with your imaginary egotistical "self." Only once you let go of that illusion are you free to do what you need to do without being hung up on your "self."

You need to be fully open and honest about yourself, while avoiding being self-absorbed in either a positive or negative way. Just accept yourself for who you are, and don't get hung up on it. Once again, it's important to remember, as the Buddha taught, that "you" are not a self-contained "thing," but an ever-changing process of interaction between mental and physical energy states.

When you admit your powerlessness and turn your life over to your Higher Consciousness, you begin to let go of any notion that you have a "self" to feel bad about. Rather than trying to develop a positive image of your "self," you let go of your self-image altogether and just let yourself be as you are, guided by your Buddha Nature. Thus by letting your Higher Consciousness guide your life, you gradually learn to yield your self-will to that consciousness.

A major lesson we've learned by this time is that you and I are not the beings we've pretended to be until now, egos existing in our own right. For we have no long-term existence apart from our Buddha Nature, who is the real Power in our lives. Now it's time to use prayer and meditation to communicate more deeply with that Higher Self to find our true meaning in life. This brings us to Step Eleven.

STEP ELEVEN: WE SEEK THROUGH BOTH PRAYER AND MEDITATION TO IMPROVE OUR CONSCIOUS CONTACT WITH OUR HIGHER CONSCIOUSNESS, AS BEST WE UNDERSTAND THIS CONSCIOUSNESS. WE PRAY ONLY FOR KNOWLEDGE OF WHAT OUR HIGHER CONSCIOUSNESS WANTS US TO DO, AND FOR THE POWER TO CARRY THAT OUT

As in the original version, we're saying "prayer AND meditation," not "prayer OR meditation." I think of prayer as verbal contemplation, and meditation as nonverbal contemplation. Step Eleven implies we need both. We need to address ourselves openly to our Higher Consciousness, and we need to listen in the silence for the unspoken Truth that can never be fully communicated through words alone.

Historically nearly all Buddhists have prayed in some form or another: chanting the sutras, taking refuge in the Three Treasures, and taking the precepts. Yet not all Buddhists meditate, even though that was probably the Buddha's original intention. No doubt the same could be said for people of all faiths. We all may be quick to address our concerns to our chosen deities, but not so quick to listen for the unspoken wisdom we could receive from that source.

Both prayer and meditation are often misunderstood. In both cases the misunderstanding is frequently along the line of expecting something supernatural to happen. Prayer is widely misused to try to manipulate the universe into giving us what we want. This is just another example of what we call "self-will run riot." In fact, there are all kinds of popularized forms of "religion" that teach us to use prayer to try to impose our own will on the universe.

Even if this scheme worked sometimes— and in my experience it rarely does, leaving its practitioners to make up all kinds of excuses for its lack of success—it merely reinforces the false notion of ego gratification. We're still assuming that we have a "self" that can impose its will on the universe. In the long run such "prayer" could actually deepen our addictive tendencies.

Step Eleven offers a clear alternative to this superstitious form of prayer. We pray not to try to rearrange the external details of our lives, but to spiritually transform ourselves. You are the only person in the universe whom you can change.

Though not all Buddhist denominations encourage meditation, most of those that encourage it also teach how to do it. There's an art to being able to sit quietly doing nothing, especially in our fast-paced modern world. As the Zen saying goes, "Don't just do something, sit there!"

Meditation is also frequently misunderstood; and in this case the problem is often one of being overly obsessed with posture or technique. Sometimes it's implied that the closer we can come to a lotus posture, the more effective and "spiritual" our meditation will be. Most likely in the Buddha's day people did ordinarily sit cross-legged on the ground.

But today most of us are accustomed to sitting in chairs; and there's no reason why we can't meditate in chairs if we can sit more comfortably that way. Of course it's helpful if we can find furniture that encourages us to keep an erect posture. Whether we sit on a cushion or in a chair, sitting erect is healthy for the body and helps us remain aware and attentive at all times, especially during meditation.

Other than that, in my experience it seems to make little difference what posture I use, how I hold my hands, or where I place my feet. I like to think of meditation as an experience I can create anytime, anywhere, so long as I can find a little time to spare.

If you tell yourself you need a special cushion to meditate, it becomes another attachment. This will give you a ready-made excuse not to meditate if you don't have that cushion handy. Besides, you may be tempted all the more to expect something magical to happen.

As with prayer, there's nothing supernatural about meditation. Your cares won't miraculously dissolve, and you probably won't see God before your eyes. It's just a chance to sit quietly and reflect, and in that silence to discern your Buddha Nature's will for your life.

In order to quiet the mind, it's a good idea to give it something to do. In some Buddhist teachings we're encouraged to watch our breathing. This isn't to imply there's something magical about breathing; it's just to keep the mind occupied.

Since there's nothing else going on, the breath is a good thing to notice in the here-and-now.

Some schools recommend use of a mantra, like "Om" or "Mu." These are fine so long as you don't expect some kind of magical result from meditating on a certain sound. The important thing is to be mindful of the present moment during each second, and to bring your mind back to the present each time it strays. One way to do this is to silently say, "Thinking!" each time your mind wanders. Thus you note the here-and-now process of thinking itself rather than getting lost in the content of your thoughts.

In the Metta Sutta the Buddha is quoted as saying we need to learn to practice meditation while standing, walking, sitting, or lying down. While most Buddhist sanghas emphasize mainly the sitting and walking meditation, I think most of us could benefit from learning to meditate in all four postures.

Standing meditation is similar to sitting, with the spine erect. Sometimes you can give yourself a break from sitting meditation by standing up for a while. This is also a good practice in public places, such as while waiting in line or participating in a vigil.

. Usually standing meditation is of relatively short duration; but it can help you find your calm center during tense or boring moments. You can lean against a wall if you absolutely must; but be sure you're erect and motionless, with your weight equally distributed on both feet. Keep noticing your breathing at all times.

Walking meditation is a little more relaxing, and can be done for a longer period of time. You can start out very slowly, noting each step. In addition to your breathing, notice how your foot feels as it contacts the ground, first the heel, then the whole foot, and then the toe as you move forward. Once in a while it's nice to practice this barefoot. After a while you can speed it up if you like, possibly even jogging or walking fast while meditating.

Be aware of your surroundings at all times while doing walking meditation. Not only is this necessary for safety, but it also helps your mindfulness practice as it keeps your mind in the here and now. Stop walking anytime you want to admire the view.

When I've done long meditation walks through the mountains I note every rock, plant or animal as I pass it. A meditation hike can be a joy, either alone or in a group; provided it's done in silence. Be careful to focus your mind on the walk itself, rather than allowing yourself to be distracted by thoughts about the past or the future.

Meditating while lying down is mainly taught to people with physical limitations, to whom it's a special blessing. Yet it need not be limited to infirm people. I practice this every day, myself, especially in the morning and at night. It's nice to meditate under a quilt or in a sleeping bag on a cold morning.

Of course this works well only if you can keep awake. Keeping your mind on the present helps you stay alert. Whatever posture you use, meditation is the gentle art of keeping the mind in the here and now.

Step Eleven corresponds to Right Contemplation in the Eightfold Path. At least once a day each one of us needs to freely and openly address our concerns in Prayer to our Higher Consciousness. And then we need to listen to the unspoken Truth as it comes to us in meditation.

As in all the steps, journal work is essential here. If we commit our prayers in writing, we can listen and see what thoughts come to us. And if we're very quiet inside as well as out, we may be able to hear the silent Divine reply.

Step Eleven ends by saying we must pray only for knowledge of what our Higher Consciousness wants us to do, and for the power to carry that out. There's no room in this system for dictating to our Higher Consciousness how we want our lives to be. The purpose of prayer and meditation, regardless of our religious affiliation, is to open ourselves to the Dharma. If we actually follow this, it gives us an opportunity to set aside our ego agendas and listen to the voice of our Buddha Nature.

As for "the power to carry that out," none of us in our egotistical mind has that power; otherwise we wouldn't need to be in recovery. We admitted in Step One that we are powerless over this area of our lives that is causing us trouble. Only our Higher Consciousness can give us the strength to fulfill our recovery—now that we've gotten our egos out of the way and let our Buddha Nature express itself.

Once our minds are focused on the Dharma, we begin to open to the awareness of our true nature. We begin to realize that, rather than the silly, craving egos we've imagined ourselves to be, we're at one with our Higher Consciousness. This awakening brings us to Step Twelve.

STEP TWELVE: HAVING FOLLOWED THESE STEPS AS AN INTEGRAL PART OF OUR SPIRITUAL PRACTICE, WE IN TIME EXPERIENCE A SPIRITUAL AWAKENING AS WE REUNITE WITH OUR HIGHER CONSCIOUSNESS. IN GRATITUDE, WE GENTLY MAKE THIS MESSAGE AVAILABLE TO OTHERS IN NEED OF RECOVERY, AS WE PRACTICE THESE PRINCIPLES IN ALL AREAS OF OUR LIVES

While I've met some people who've chosen to make the Twelve Steps their only spiritual path, more often the process is to work the steps in conjunction with our own religion, be it Buddhism, Christianity, or whatever. The steps are meant to be harmonious with most traditional religions, Buddhism as well as Christianity.

If we continue to meditate and pray, as Steps Eleven and Twelve suggest, in time we will have a Spiritual Awakening in some form or other. This may or may not mean a White Light experience such as Bill W. had, but it does mean a transcendental experience of great joy as we realize we're not stuck in the little boxes in which we've been confining ourselves.

In the early days of A.A., Bill W. and his friends quickly discovered that the more they worked to bring the steps to other alcoholics, the less likely they themselves were to backslide. This is true in all the Twelve Step programs. Making the work of recovery available to other addicts is an important part of one's own recovery.

I myself have benefited from having a sponsor in my program. My past sponsors have assured me they got as much out of sponsoring me as I did in working with them. Now I want to offer myself as a sponsor to others, partly out of gratitude, but also because I'm convinced it's the best way to keep myself in recovery. Also, writing this book has been an invaluable Twelfth-Step exercise.

The very act of giving your time to help others offers an excellent opportunity to get beyond your absorption with your "self" and realize your oneness with the Universe. This is what Mahayana Buddhists call the Path of the Bodhisattva: selfless living and selfless giving. In this process we find our spiritual awakening.

The sutras say the Buddha found enlightenment alone, meditating under a fig tree. So delighted was he that he spent days and nights in ecstasy there. Then it occurred to him that he might share his discover with others.

According to one version, Mara, the devil, who had earlier tried to talk him out of meditating there in the first place, now reversed course and advised him to remain in bliss under the fig tree and not bother to share his enlightenment with anyone else, since no one would understand anyway. The Buddha considered this, but decided in the end that there might be at least some people who would understand. Thus he left the tree and Mara behind to go out into the world and teach others.

Of course Mara was never meant to be thought of as an incarnation of evil, but rather the personification of illusion. This shows that even after being enlightened, the Buddha felt tempted to think only of himself. But then he realized that he couldn't go on being an enlightened being by himself; he HAD to share his knowledge with others, even if few would truly understand. Mahayana Buddhists might take it a step further and say the Buddha would not have been truly enlightened unless he felt determined to assist others in their own journeys to enlightenment.

Perhaps you and I might be stretching a point to compare ourselves with the Buddha. Still, we have no more right than he to think we can do our spiritual journey alone. If Buddha, Jesus, and Bill W. all felt it was essential to share their enlightenment experiences with others, then you and I have no acceptable alternative but to do likewise.

I've changed the wording of this step a bit to remind us that we don't want to get pushy when we offer the program to other addicts. Yet most of us are more likely to err in the opposite direction. We may become shy or lazy when we could be there for others who need us.

Finally, we resolve to practice these principles in all areas of our lives. The original wording, still widely in use, says, "in all our affairs." This is harmless enough, unless you happen to be a recovering sex addict and want to stop having affairs altogether; at least the wrong kind of affairs. In most sexual recovery programs the word "affairs" is changed to something else; and thus we do so here.

What's important here is that we don't compartmentalize our spirituality or our recovery. That's why so many of us who have all along attended church or temple have still found ourselves caught up in addiction. The problem wasn't necessarily with the particular religious tradition we practiced, but that we walled it off from our everyday life. Sunday morning we went to church or our meditation group; then on Sunday evening we got smashed, got laid, went low-riding, gambled all night, spent all our savings, or watched television until dawn the next morning.

Many hunting and gathering cultures have no word for "religion" in their languages. This isn't because the people aren't religious; they invariably are. In such cultures spirituality is so integrated with everyday life that it permeates everyone's existence on a moment-to-moment basis. In our fast-paced, overly compartmentalized urban life, many of us could benefit from a dose of such folk wisdom. In any case the Twelve Steps, like all valid forms of spirituality, are meant to be practiced every moment, "in all areas of our lives."

The Buddha never intended to create a religion to be practiced once a week, or even once a day; he offered a spiritual practice to be engaged in every moment. That's why the Eightfold Path offers so many principles we are to practice on a moment-to-moment basis. That is the path that leads to Spiritual Awakening. The Four Noble Truths and the Twelve Steps simply offer different guidebooks to the same Path; the same is true of other spiritual traditions.

In teaching that there is no eternal, unchanging soul, the Buddha was pointing out that each of us is a process, not a static entity. While you may have been an addict all of your adult life, there may also have been moments when your addictions didn't trouble you especially. There may finally come a time when you no longer need to identify yourself as an addict. Or at least, instead of forever identifying yourself as a RECOVERING addict, you may identify yourself as a RECOVERED addict.

True, you may still be in potential danger of falling back into previous or new addictive patterns if you fail to confront the realities of life. Yet as long as you live honestly and openly, your former addictions need no longer control you. This is the process you and I have been working toward all along: letting go of our self-centered egotistical concept of "self," and opening ourselves to the only being that has permanent existence, our unselfish Higher Consciousness.

CONCLUSION

Now let's summarize the Four Noble Truths, and then the Twelve Steps.

THE FIRST NOBLE TRUTH: Life by its very nature is unsatisfactory, and suffering is found everywhere. Each of us is powerless over many aspects of our own lives, not to mention the rest of the world, sometimes to the extent that our lives are out of control. All of us will experience pain and sorrow, and in time we will all grow old, become infirm, and die. When we leave everything up to our individual wills, we commonly perform actions that create more and more suffering for ourselves and others. Thus, suffering is found everywhere, and nearly everyone experiences it. In short, life is a bitch, and then you die!

THE SECOND NOBLE TRUTH: The reason all of us suffer is that, due to our ignorant nature, we're obsessed with self-centered, addictive craving for what we don't have, as well as clinging to what we do have. In the end our very efforts to seek more and more satisfaction for ourselves are certain to create more suffering for ourselves and others.

THE THIRD NOBLE TRUTH: In order to overcome suffering we must let go of this addictive, egotistical identity of ours and learn to live unselfishly and without attachment, thus allowing ourselves to be absorbed into the Emptiness of NIRVANA.

THE FOURTH NOBLE TRUTH: There is a way out of our addictive craving that leads to complete liberation from suffering. Based on correct understanding and aspiration, rigorous ethical self-discipline, and effortful and mindful contemplation, the way out of suffering is called the Eightfold Path. The eight aspects of this Path are Right Understanding, Right Aspiration, Right Speech, Right Action, Right Livelihood, Right Effort, Right Mindfulness, and Right Concentration.

Now once again, the Twelve Steps:

STEP ONE: We admit that, identified with our egotistical "selves," we are powerless over our human weaknesses; to the extent that at times we've been unable to manage our own lives.

STEP TWO: We become aware of a Consciousness far greater than our egotistical "selves" that can restore us to wholeness.

STEP THREE: We make a decision to return our lives and our will to the care of this Consciousness greater than our "selves," as best we understand this Consciousness.

STEP FOUR: We honestly and painstakingly examine ourselves as we really are, sparing no details, however embarrassing.

STEP FIVE: We admit to our Higher Consciousness, to ourselves, and to another safe and sympathetic human being the exact nature of our personal weaknesses.

STEP SIX: We become entirely ready to allow our Higher Consciousness to work with us to transform all our personal weaknesses into strengths.

STEP SEVEN: We wholeheartedly invite our Higher Consciousness to work with us to transform all of our personal weaknesses into strengths.

STEP EIGHT: We make a list of all the persons whom we have harmed in our lives, including, most likely, ourselves; and we become ready to make amends to them all. We also list those persons who have harmed us, and we consider what it would take for us to forgive them completely.

STEP NINE: When possible we try to make direct amends to everyone whom we have harmed (including ourselves), except when doing so might cause further damage to them, to ourselves, or to someone else. In addition, we make a conscientious effort to forgive everyone who has harmed us.

STEP TEN: We continue to be mindfully aware of all our motives and actions. When we make a mistake, we promptly admit it and resolve to do better from now on. At the same time, we accept ourselves fully and reaffirm our basic worth as human beings.

STEP ELEVEN: We seek through both prayer and meditation to improve our conscious contact with our Higher Consciousness, as best we understand this Power. We pray only for better understanding of our Higher Consciousness's will for us, and for the strength to carry that out.

STEP TWELVE: Having followed these steps as an integral part of our spiritual practice, we in time experience a spiritual awakening as we reunite with our Higher Consciousness. In gratitude, we now gently make this message available to others in need of recovery, as we practice these principles in all areas of our lives.

We've seen that the cause of our suffering lies not merely in external events, but in our own thoughts and actions, based on our false concept of ourselves as independent entities. Turning our lives over to our Higher Consciousness constitutes letting go of that self-image, to recognize our oneness with the Emptiness of Ultimate Being.

Mystics of all religions have said that the way to find Spiritual Awakening is to open ourselves completely through prayer and meditation, and listen to the still inner voice. Then in Divine Ecstasy, when the distinction between our Higher Consciousness and ourselves disappears, it does so not because we absorb that Consciousness into ourselves, but because we put aside our illusory idea of "self" and become absorbed in the Divine Emptiness completely. This is the spiritual Awakening of which both Bill W. and the Buddha spoke.

ANNOTATED BIBLIOGRAPHY

Alcoholics Anonymous
TWELVE STEPS AND TWELVE TRADITIONS
Alcoholics Anonymous World Service, New York, 1981
Commonly known as "Twelve and Twelve," this is a description of the twelve steps and twelve traditions used by AA and other Twelve Step groups.

William Alexander
COOL WATER
ALCOHOLISM, MINDFULNESS, AND ORDINARY RECOVERY
Shambhala Publications, Boston, 1997
The founder of the Ordinary Recovery movement explains how to use Buddhist principles in recovery from addiction. As a Buddhist, a Christian, and a recovered alcoholic, Mr. Alexander speaks from dramatic personal experience.

Mel Ash
THE ZEN OF RECOVERY
Jeremy P. Tarcher/Putnam, New York, 1993
This is the original Zen "Big Book" of recovery from addiction, used by Buddhist-oriented Twelve Step meetings nationwide. While primarily from a Zen and A. A. perspective, it's valuable for all people in recovery.

Melody Beattie
CODEPENDENTS' GUIDE TO THE TWELVE STEPS
HOW TO FIND THE RIGHT PROGRAM FOR YOU AND APPLY EACH OF THE TWELVE STEPS TO YOUR OWN ISSUES
Fireside, New York, 1990
A founder of CODA goes through the Twelve Steps one by one, adapting and applying each one to the special needs of codependents.

Thomas Bien, PhD., and Beverly Bien, M.Ed.
MINDFUL RECOVERY
A SPIRITUAL PATH TO RECOVERY FROM ADDICTION
Foreword by G. Alan Marlatt, PhD.
J. Wiley and Sons, New York, 2002
The Biens draw on Buddhism among other religions to offer their "Ten Doorways to Mindful Recovery" as either a supplement or an alternative to the Twelve Steps.

Venerable Bikkhu Bodhi
THE NOBLE EIGHTFOLD PATH
THE WAY TO THE END OF SUFFERING
Buddhist Publication Society, Sri Lanka, 1994
An American-born Theravada monk explains Buddha's Eightfold Path thoroughly and in precise detail.

Patrick J. Carnes, PhD.
A GENTLE PATH THROUGH THE TWELVE STEPS
FOR ALL PEOPLE IN THE PROCESS OF RECOVERY
Hazelden Educational Materials, Center City, Minnesota, 1994
This is one of a series of books on recovery from addiction written by a prominent psychologist who has devoted his life to studying it.

Venerable Pema Chodron
WHEN THINGS FALL APART
HEART ADVICE FOR DIFFICULT TIMES
Shambhala, Boston, 1997
A prominent American-born Vajrayana Buddhist nun explains how we can use the adverse circumstances we all face in life to work toward personal liberation.

His Holiness the Dalai Lama
THE FOUR NOBLE TRUTHS
FUNDAMENTALS OF THE BUDDHIST TEACHINGS
Translated by Geshe Thupten Jinpa
Edited by Dominique Side
Thorson, London, 1997
This is a transcription of a series of Dharma talks by His Holiness on the basic Buddhist principles, including the Four Noble Truths and the Eightfold Path.

Tian Dayton, PhD.
TRAUMA AND ADDICTION
ENDING THE CYCLE OF PAIN THROUGH EMOTIONAL LITERACY
Heath Communications, Deerfield Beach, FL, 2000.
A clinical psychologist details how and why trauma leads to addiction, and how to make peace with the past and overcome the addictive cycle.

Lance M. Dodes, M.D.
THE HEART OF ADDICTION
HarperCollins, New York, 2002
In this book Dr. Dodes offers valuable insight into the ways in which feeling of powerlessness can drive people to a variety of types of addictive behavior.

Kevin Griffin, *ONE BREATH AT A TIME*
BUDDHISM AND THE TWELVE STEPS
Rodale Press, 2004
Meditation teacher Griffin explains how the Twelve Steps of AA assisted his Buddhist practice while helping him overcome his alcoholism.

Christina Grof
THE SEARCH FOR WHOLENESS
ATTACHMENT, ADDICTION, AND THE SPIRITUAL PATH
Harper San Francisco, 1994
Grof shares her own experiences with alcoholism, Twelve-Step recovery programs, transpersonal psychology, and Buddhist thought.

Cheri Huber
THE KEY
AND THE NAME OF THE KEY IS
WILLINGNESS
Keep It Simple Books, Murphys, CA, 1998
A Zen teacher offers clear, practical advice on self-acceptance, in a format that is easy to follow.

Charlotte Davis Kasl, PhD.
MANY ROADS, ONE JOURNEY
MOVING BEYOND THE TWELVE
STEPS
HarperCollins, New York, 1992
Dr. Kasl is a psychologist who specializes in working with people in recovery. She presents a fascinating approach to recovery, rooted in feminism and social awareness.

Kate Kelly and Peggy Raimundo
YOU MEAN I'M NOT LAZY, STUPID, OR CRAZY?!
A SELF-HELP BOOK FOR ADULTS WITH ATTENTION DEFICIT DISORDER
Foreword by Larry B. Silver, M. D.
Simon and Schuster, New York, 1993
This is an excellent guidebook for adults suffering from attention deficit disorder.

Ken Keyes, Jr.
HANDBOOK TO HIGHER CONSCIOUS-NESS
Living Love Press, Berkeley, CA, 1976
This book shows us how to find happiness by upgrading our addictions into preferences.

Ananda Maitreya, translator
THE DHAMMAPA
THE PATH OF TRUTH
Foreword by Ven. Thich Nhat Hanh
Parallax Press, Berkeley, CA, 1995
This is a clear, pocket-sized paperback translation of the classic Buddhist text.

Harvey Milkman and Stanley G. Sunderwirth
CRAVING FOR ECSTASY
HOW PASSIONS BECOME ADDICTIONS, AND WHAT WE CAN DO ABOUT THEM
Jossey-Bass Publishers, San Francisco, 1998
This book discusses the latest psychological findings on addiction.

Venerable Thich Nhat Hanh
THE HEART OF THE BUDDHA'S TEACHING
TRANSFORMING SUFFERING INTO PEACE, JOY, AND LIBERATION
Parallax Press, Berkeley, CA, 1998
A famous Zen monk and poet explains in simple terms the basic Buddhist teachings.

ANNOTATED BIBLIOGRAPHY

Venerable Walpola Sri Rahula, PhD.
WHAT THE BUDDHA TAUGHT
Grove Wiedenfeld, New York, 1974
A Prominent Sri Lankan Theravada Buddhist monk and scholar examines the basic teachings of the Buddha, including the Four Noble Truths and the Eightfold Path.

Ronald A. Ruder and Marcia Byalick
THE CRAVING BRAIN
A BOLD NEW APPROACH TO BREAKING FREE FROM DRUG ADDICTION, OVEREATING, AND ALCOHOLISM
HarperCollins, New York, 1997
This book discusses the medical aspects of addiction.

Laura S., *12 STEPS ON BUDDHA'S PATH*
BILL, BUDDHA, AND WE
Foreword by Sylvia Boorstein
Wisdom Publications, 2006
A recovering alcoholic describes how AA and Buddhism worked together to facilitate her recovery

Rev. Koshin Schomberg
DEPENDENT ORIGINATION
North Cascades Buddhist Priory, McKenna, WA, 1999
A Zen monk explains how "The teaching of "Dependent Origination is a detailed explanation of the First and Second of Buddha's Four Noble Truths."

Venerable Ajahn Sumedho
THE FOUR NOBLE TRUTHS
Amaravati Publications, Hertfordshire, England, 1992
An American-born Theravada Buddhist monk and teacher explains the basic Buddhist teachings of the Four Noble Truths.

Joseph Volpicelli, M.D., PhD. and Maia Szalavitz
RECOVERY OPTIONS
THE COMPLETE GUIDE
John Wiley and Sons, New York, 2000
This book provides a modern look at alcoholism and drug addiction.

Dr. Kimberly S. Young
CAUGHT IN THE NET
HOW TO RECOGNIZE THE SIGNS OF INTERNET ADDICTION—AND A WINNING STRATEGY OF RECOVERY
John Wiley and Sons, New York, 1998
This book discusses the growing problem of Internet addiction and what to do about it.